P9-DEF-302

BOOKS BY DOROTHY RODGERS

The House in My Head

My Favorite Things

DOROTHY RODGERS

THE HOUSE IN MY HEAD

AVENEL BOOKS • NEW YORK

The photographs in *The House in My Head* were produced by *House Beautiful* Magazine, which followed the building of the house from its inception. They are used here through the courtesy of the magazine. All photographs, unless otherwise credited in the list of Illustrations, were taken by Ezra Stoller.

I wish to express my appreciation to Pearl Magyar for her enthusiastic interest in the house and for her patience in testing the appliances; to the friends who contributed recipes; and to Anna Muffoletto for testing the recipes given in this book.

Dorothy Rodgers

517118831

Library of Congress catalog card number 67-25491

This edition is published by Avenel Books
a division of Crown Publishers, Inc.
by arrangement with Atheneum
a b c d e f g h
Manufactured in the United States of America

Contents

ACKNOWLEDGMENT

After two books, Marcia Wallace still stands near the top of my list of favorite people. She has worked closely with me with patience, wit and understanding and has helped me to organize and edit my tales of woe and cries of delight into this book.

THE HOUSE IN MY HEAD

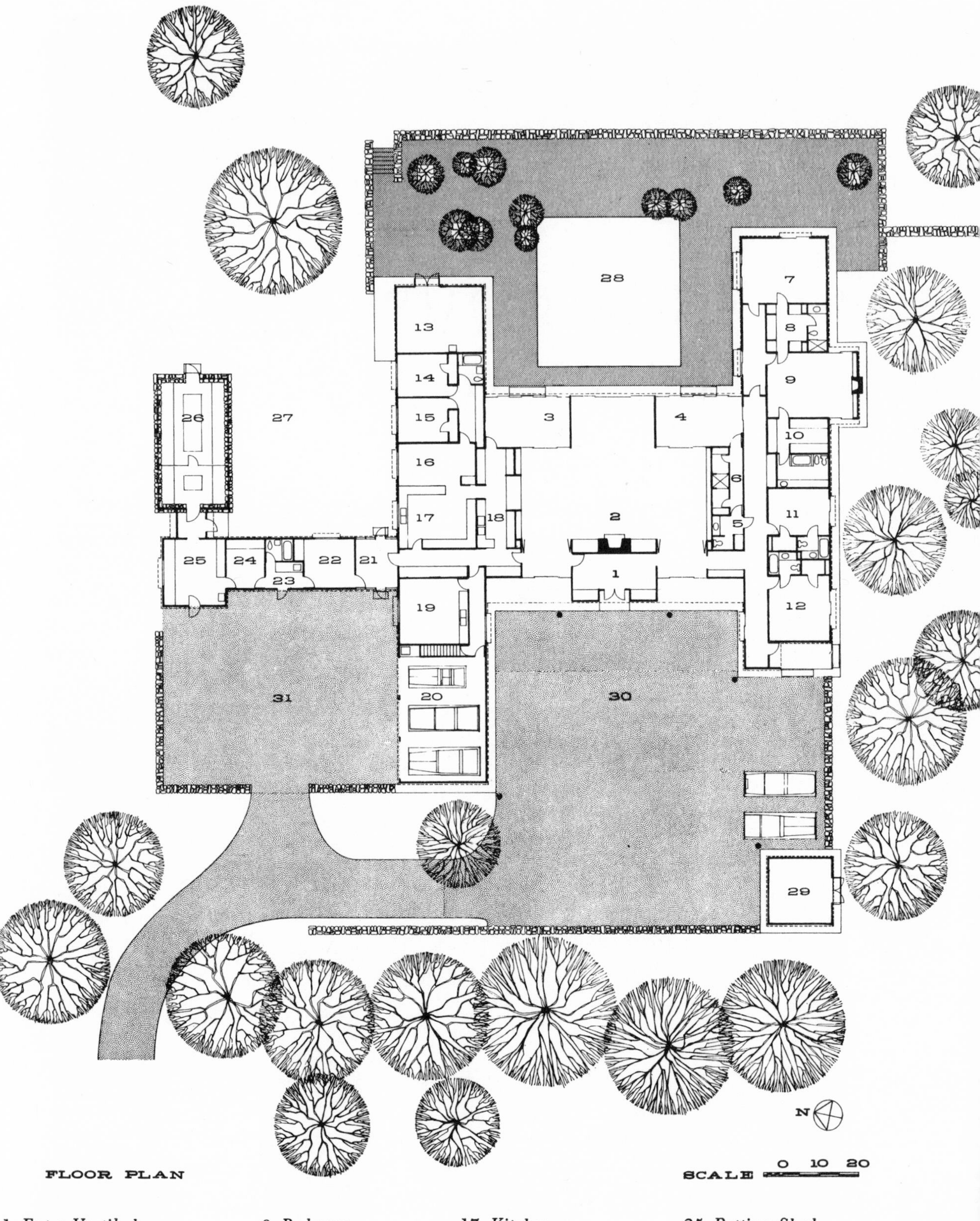

1 *Entry Vestibule*
2 *Living Room*
3 *Dining Porch*
4 *Sitting Porch*
5 *Powder Room*
6 *Pool Dressing Rooms*
7 *Bedroom*
8 *Dressing Room*
9 *Bedroom*
10 *Dressing Room*
11 *Bedroom*
12 *Bedroom*
13 *Storage*
14 *Maid's Room*
15 *Maid's Room*
16 *Kitchen Sitting*
17 *Kitchen*
18 *Pantry*
19 *Laundry*
20 *Garage*
21 *Porch*
22 *Caretaker's Room*
23 *Galley*
24 *Storage*
25 *Potting Shed*
26 *Greenhouse*
27 *Garden*
28 *Pool*
29 *Storage*
30 *Entrance Courtyard*
31 *Service Courtyard*

June 1965

EVEN while I was working on the manuscript of *My Favorite Things*, I think I really knew that we were not going to be able to continue to live at Rockmeadow in the way we had always enjoyed. For sixteen years the big traditional colonial house in Southport, Connecticut, with its sunny rooms and beautiful gardens, had been home in the country for Dick and me. But keeping it going smoothly was becoming impossibly complicated. I had always wanted to build a house, and suddenly I felt sure that this was the moment.

For Dick, as for most men, change is at best uninviting, even when the end result is an improvement. To decide to leave anything as lovely as Rockmeadow, a house to which we had given so much love and care and thought, was extremely painful. It probably seemed to Dick like selling one of our daughters, and he was also worried that it might take years before a new house could be built. For weeks he went around looking like a wounded deer.

All of our friends reacted in the same way to our decision to build: astonishment and dismay at the thought of our selling Rockmeadow followed quite rapidly by complete understanding of the problems involved in trying to run it. Then came the Cassandra-like predictions of the trouble we would have in building and dire warnings about costs. But after all the somber prophecies there was enthusiasm and, I sensed in many of our friends, a kind of longing to build houses of their own.

For years I had been storing up ideas: now I would have a chance to use them. Nothing like the house I had in mind existed, because it was to be planned for the way we like to live. There are approximations, of course, but they are hard to find in the northeastern part of the United States because relatively few custom-designed contemporary houses have been built there. There are some beautiful ones in California and Florida, in Texas and Hawaii and in many other states, but conditions of climate and topography bring their own built-in attractions or problems—in each case very different from the charms and drawbacks of New England.

The house in my head is not only real, it is practical, comfortable, easy to maintain, beautiful, and it works. And this book will be about building, furnishing and—finally—living in it.

I realize that very few people build from the beginning as we are doing. But even if you are only remodeling a kitchen or a bathroom, I hope you will be able to make use of some of the ideas we find helpful.

In the pages to come, I will tell you about our experiences: the things I discover in planning and decorating our new house. I hope its design will make possible an informal way of entertaining that we could never have managed at Rockmeadow, and that this, in turn, will suggest new kinds of parties you might enjoy giving. *My Favorite Things* was about the past and the present. *The House in My Head* is about the present and the future. I'll be writing it as it happens, and unless I cheat, I won't know how it comes out any more than you.

CHAPTER ONE

From the Ground Up

THE camel's back broke on Memorial Day in 1965 when, for a few desperate hours, it looked as though we would be left just at the start of summer without a couple to help at Rockmeadow. This time, I felt, things could only get worse. And our daughter Mary, who knows a last straw when she sees one, said, "You really ought to sell the place—now—and build yourselves the house you want, one that would be much easier to take care of." Sadly, I realized she was right.

For sixteen years Rockmeadow had been our home in the country, a place to relax with friends in the summer and a place where Dick and I could get away by ourselves for weekends the rest of the year. In a way, it felt more like home than our city apartment, although, in fact, we spent more time in New York. Perhaps it was because we gave so much to Rockmeadow. We worked on it, cared for it, loved it. In return it had given us tremendous pleasure. But gradually it had become too much to cope with.

I have to admit that this was our fault: we had complicated

life for ourselves there. The family who'd had the place before us had three children and loved the riding and hunting for which Fairfield County is famous. The Fairfield Hunt rode over the open fields, and there was even a skeet range in the back meadow. Rockmeadow's former owners spent a good deal of time at the Hunt Club down the road. Like most year-round residents, they had very few weekend guests, and they did most of their entertaining with cocktail parties or dinners at the Club. So the house and grounds ran comfortably with relatively little help.

We had changed Rockmeadow indoors and out to suit our quite different lives. Rooms that had been family bedrooms were guest rooms for us. We added another bathroom. And because we like to entertain at home, we had enlarged the pantry (doing away with a breakfast room in the process) and put in a more modern kitchen. We had made all sorts of gardens because we love flowers; we built a caretaker's cottage and a greenhouse, and turned the meadow, where horses had been pastured, into a croquet field.

When we'd finished, we had a house that, while not huge itself, took huge amounts of tending. The areas to be looked after were endless. Inside there was brass to be polished, black wooden floors to be waxed, three flights of stairs and halls to be dusted and, as in any old-fashioned house, all sorts of actually unused space to be cleaned. Outdoors there were lawns to mow, the driveway to rake, hedges and edges to trim. We had several garden areas for looking and one large one for cutting, all of them requiring weeding and pruning. And the weekend entertaining we enjoyed so much—house guests and friends who came out for the day to swim or have lunch or play croquet—meant trays to be carried, luggage to be taken upstairs (I never felt it was very welcoming to ask just-arrived guests to drag their own things up to the third floor) and meals to be served—seated, since neither the dining room nor the terrace lent itself very gracefully to buffets. We really asked for trouble, and we got it.

Being weekend residents, we had to depend on a couple who would live on the place the year round to keep things functioning smoothly. Such people were increasingly hard to find and, once found, more and more difficult for me to keep in close touch with. Life got busier, and Dick and I were able to get up for fewer weekends between fall and spring. Even when we found ourselves free in winter, the deteriorating railroad service made us hesitate. When we had first moved to Fairfield County, trains were frequent, they ran on time and they were clean. And when we went up on Fridays, which we did regularly every other week, we never felt we could be trapped by the weather. There was always a train that would get us back to the city. These days that isn't true. And Dick, who hates driving on icy roads, doesn't dare find himself snowed in and unable to keep Monday appointments in town.

As our winter weekends at Rockmeadow became less frequent, I lost some of my on-the-spot feel about how things were going there. I worried, with reason, about help staying on. And even when things seemed to be moving fairly smoothly, I would arrive on a Friday barely ahead of guests, to be greeted by a list of things that needed attention. Usually it was too late to get repair people to come that day. No one wanted to work on Saturday or Sunday. On Monday I'd make phone calls to set the wheels in motion, then have to leave for town with a slightly guilty feeling at not having left things quite right. So subtly that we were hardly conscious of its happening, Rockmeadow had become more and more costly, emotionally as well as financially. The time came when I simply didn't have the energy to run it as we had. Sensibly, someone else might have given up guests or allowed the gardens to de-landscape themselves. But these were part of our Rockmeadow life, and we couldn't. For us, as Mary said, starting over was the only logical solution.

The Decision to Build

It was a very difficult decision to make—especially for Dick. Looking back, I realized that I had seen the handwriting on the wall, but he had been less conscious than I that a move was inevitable. Leaving anything as lovely as Rockmeadow was a tremendous wrench, and he resisted with all his might. But he finally came to feel that it was the right thing to do.

From the beginning, I seemed to know what I wanted the new house to be. Sitting in the garden that fall of 1965, I thought, sentimentally, how beautiful Rockmeadow was with the leaves beginning to turn, and I knew there was one trap I would have to avoid: that of trying to build another Rockmeadow. There could never be anything lovelier. But basically we needed a place that would be much easier to run, less dependent on live-in help, a place we could open and close for winter weekends without having to have a caretaker all year round. More efficient planning, fewer levels and less manicured landscaping could take the worry out of upkeep and give us again a place that would be fun to live in.

Since this was to be a house to enjoy, I didn't want to postpone living in it one unnecessary minute. Once our minds were made up, I felt the sooner we moved the better. Besides, if I let myself get much older, I might not have the courage to build a house from scratch.

I say "from scratch," but when we began to discuss the new place seriously, I discovered there was already a house in my head. I don't know how long it had been there. But I have my own theory about it. Psychologists say everyone is born with a fear of loud noises and falling. I think everyone is born with a desire to build a house. The smallest child, left to his own devices on a beach, builds a sand castle; given paper and a crayon, he'll draw himself a house complete with chimney smoke and flowers. Then there's a table that, blanket-covered, becomes a tent he can crawl into, or a tree house—a place that is all his own. Once shelter has been taken care of, he starts making improvements, substituting a proper ladder for boards nailed to the tree trunk, adding a shelf or a box for supplies. Next comes paint or a flowerpot just because it looks nice. My point is that no house springs full-blown, that even one as sophisticated, as beautiful and efficient as Jefferson's Monticello may have had its start on a Virginia beach.

At any rate, there—already begun—was the house in my head. I discovered that parts of plans existed on paper. As I sorted out things at Rockmeadow and in the apartment, I found a notebook dated July 1963 with entries about a possible magazine piece. "Can't stop thinking about building a house," it said. "Eleven-foot ceilings and tall doors and windows where possible. . . . Why must rooms be squared off? Why not pentagonal or hexagonal? Perhaps it might work for an entrance hall or a passageway. . . . Think in terms of areas. Entertaining. Sleeping area with access to service area. . . . Dick's bedroom, workroom (?). . . ." Notes and lists went on from there.

Undoubtedly it sounds strange, but there was not much description of how the new house would look. Although I have always been drawn to indigenous materials—the travertine in Rome, the white marble of Greece, Jerusalem's honey-colored stone—and I love the rugged look of fieldstone in New England, I had never given the house in my head a specific kind of "skin." As far as shape was concerned, I could survey the Connecticut countryside and see a great deal of what I didn't want in the rising crop of Colonials and saltboxes, all adaptations, all done with so little thought about living in the 1960's. I admire the grace of Versailles and the disciplined beauty of Georgian architecture, but I've never wanted to build a reproduction. The exterior restrictions: the symmetrical windows, the doors placed just so with no consideration of present need, are too rigid, too limiting. For me, contemporary architecture's freedom to design for a way of living without conforming to any pre-set style has always had a much stronger appeal. So in my 1963 notes, the rather tentative statement that I "would love to have it look a little like a Palladian villa" was followed by a very important "but." "But," said the notes, "I want to start with the inside."

In the past when we'd talked of building, Dick would sum up my feelings by saying that I wanted "a small house with large rooms and a great many of them." And, judging by early lists which included "a caretaker's apartment," the house of my notes was large and elaborate, obviously a year-round place run by just the sort of live-in servants we'd had such trouble finding. Simplifying service would reduce size and building costs considerably. Still, friends teased me about the scale of the house we were planning. It would be as big as Rockmeadow, they said, and we would still have to have servants. As far as live-in help and actual floor space were concerned, they were wrong. But we had never considered trying to do without servants, and size was not the point. What I cared about most was having a place that not only looked beautiful but worked with the least possible day-to-day care from me or from anyone else. And while I realized that building it would be expensive, the reduced cost of its upkeep would be tremendous—in terms both of money and of time saved by eliminating many housekeeping chores. I hoped that our increased pleasure would make it worth every penny we invested.

Time was important. Before June 1965 was over, Rockmeadow had been sold. And Dick, unhappy enough with the decision to move, was miserable at the thought that we might be houseless the following summer. Under the circumstances, his suggestion that we look for an existing house we could remodel seemed purest logic. And, honestly, I tried. I consulted numbers of brokers about their white elephants. I asked about guest cottages and gate lodges on estates. What we wanted, I reasoned, was a beautiful piece of land endowed with a house of no consequence, one we wouldn't mind pulling apart. Even if we could save only the foundation, we felt we would be ahead.

Yet nothing we saw seemed workable. There was a place in Greenwich with a guest house on a hill, but the main house was so big it was frightening, and the owners wouldn't divide the land. In the case of the farm just down the road from Rockmeadow, it wasn't the outdoor plumbing that put us off; it was the fact that the property was too small to provide us with the privacy we wanted. It became increasingly obvious that our onetime idea of building a house for our new life on the existing foundations of an old house we bought to tear down simply wouldn't work. As an architect friend put it, "You'd always be hemmed in by the shape of those basement walls. Besides, there'd be so much to change, it might cost you more in the end." I wanted so much to build a whole house of our own that I probably would have believed him even if I had thought he was just saying words he knew I wanted to hear.

Looking for Land

It is foolish to try to sell an existing house to anyone who wants to build one, but looking for land wasn't that much easier. We had, of course, pictured a place with magnificent trees and a great sweep of view to recommend it. But, we discovered, in our part of the world such panoramas are possible only from the heights of undeveloped land a considerable distance inland. Finding a view would probably have meant leaving the area around Southport and Fairfield where we had come to feel so at home, where we liked and trusted people like the plumber and the man who fixes the television set. We were happy with the stores and the service and our doctor. Paul Heetmann, the gardener who had grown such beautiful flowers for us for fifteen years, lived in Fairfield, and moving too far away might have meant losing him. So although we might have been tempted had we found The Perfect Spot, we were reluctant to transplant ourselves for anything less.

Besides, we had already learned that a view, by itself, cannot make the wrong land right. We had never built a house before, but, carried away by the scenery, some years earlier we had bought ourselves a hilltop in Easton, Connecticut. Panoramically speaking, we couldn't have wished for anything more spectacular. Its 360-degree view took in the foothills of the Catskills, Long Island across the Sound and—on a clear day—even the Empire State Building to the southwest. The near views were beautiful, too: small lakes and picture-book farms with grazing cows and sheep. I could see the house we'd have there crowned with a room (perhaps a second-floor study for Dick) that was literally glass all around. In my mind's eye it was perfection. In real life the property could hardly have been less practical. There wasn't enough water, and no one could say how complicated or costly digging for more might have been. We would have had to import trees and quantities of topsoil, since hilltops are notorious for losing the best of their dirt to the bottomland below. Finally, the pitch of the land was so steep that building would have been extremely expensive and reaching the house in winter would have been impossible. We might have lived with this last disadvantage, but it would have set a discouraging limit on the resale price of any house we might build. It was all too much for us to cope with, and we ended by selling the property to a very rich man who spent the cold months in Florida. He built a too, too solid house (he called it "ranch-type English") with a linen-fold paneled library, an amethyst chandelier and leaded-glass windows. He didn't care much about views.

In the course of our current search, we covered hundreds of acres. We saw one beautiful piece of land with trees I had dreamed of—great copper beeches that had grown and prospered with years of loving care. The view of the Sound was lovely, but the Thruway perspective, with accompanying traffic noise, was positively devastating. Traveling sixty miles from the city only to be deafened by rumbling trucks and train hoots seemed to make no sense at all. Another place looked as though it might have had a spectacular view if we had only been able to make our way through the underbrush. But it was virgin land, and simply preparing to build on it—bringing in a road, digging wells, clearing brush, not to mention later landscaping and planting trees—would have meant just the kind of delay we were trying so hard to avoid.

I'll always remember the real-estate man who showed us various properties and who found the one we finally bought. Respected and highly recommended, he knew everyone and every inch of land in the community. His soul was nine parts caution and one part glint in the eye. And as we toured and trudged along the Connecticut coast, our struggles to wrest a committed answer from him became a sort of game we played constantly, but never, never won. We did, however, learn something about decoding. When we asked whether a neighboring field might ever become a housing-development site, he would answer, "Anything's possible in this wicked world," which, freely translated, meant "yes." On another occasion, we said we'd heard that mosquitoes bred next door to a piece of land. "Well, to be perfectly honest," said he, "I'd have to tell you they might, but then again they might not." Somehow I felt we'd have got the same answer if we had asked about zebras. Reassurance was not in him.

And when one day he left us with a wave and a "Well, I'm off to ply my dishonest trade," an apprehensive chill went straight to my toes.

Choosing the Architect

Meanwhile, in another most important department, a very nice thing had happened: we had decided upon our architect. Friends assumed that we were planning to use a Name architect. Yet it seemed to us that a Name was the last thing we wanted. In the process of becoming famous, a Frank Lloyd Wright or a Philip Johnson or an Edward Stone develops a style by which you can recognize his work. In a public building, this very fact may mean added prestige for the city or firm that hires him. Understandably, the few private homes such men design (time and expense limit the number drastically) bear this same signature. But we think a house should be different: it should have its owners', not its designer's, stamp. Dick and I wanted this house to be ours. And, fortunately, we knew a young man who, we believed, could design it.

His name was in my 1963 notes: "I would enjoy working with John Stonehill, if he would be willing. He is gifted, young, flexible, and we have great rapport." "Gifted" is something of an understatement where John is concerned. A graduate of the Yale School of Architecture, he had won the *Prix de Rome* and spent a year studying at the American Academy there. After several years spent working for a large firm, he had joined forces with a senior partner, Oliver Lundquist. Together they had created a remarkably imaginative design for the Mount Morris Park amphitheater that was to be Dick's gift to the City of New York. And although John had never done a house, I felt sure that he would do ours beautifully.

His talent is very special. And, at the risk of being accused of nepotism, I felt that he should not be penalized for being my cousin and that it was, in fact, a real advantage. Few people building a house are lucky enough to have known their architect for any length of time. John had visited us in the city and at Rockmeadow since he was a boy. He knew us and the kind of life we live. That can make a tremendous difference.

I was delighted to have our feelings confirmed in a conversation I had some months later with the distinguished architect Max Abramovitz. Large busy firms, he told me, often have to delegate their residential work to young graduates who may or may not be especially talented. And not knowing the one assigned, you may be unable to judge whether or not he is the right architect for you. The ideal choice, Mr. Abramovitz said, would be a bright young man on his way up, preferably someone you know personally.

This is not always easy. It is hard to discover whether the genius of a house you especially like is that of the person for whom it was built or that of the man who designed it. Probably it's a combination of both. We know a couple who consulted six different firms before plans for their new house were finally completed. It was a costly enough project before they brought an architect over from Europe to help. They had learned that he'd worked on a Riviera house they'd particularly admired. Too late, they found that it was the owner, Captain Edward Molyneux, who had been the creative force. The man they'd hoped could solve all their problems had merely carried out the Captain's ideas. So that architect returned to France, and they went on with their search.

If you know no one to start with or can find no one you feel is really right, the local chapter of the American Institute of Architects is a good source of information about qualified men in your area. I stress "in your area" for two reasons. First, whether you're building a new house or remodeling an old one, it's important that the architect be on the spot to supervise construction; it can't be done by mail or telephone. Second, and even more important, he should know both the country and its climate well; they can make such a difference in the materials he chooses, not to mention such essentials as heating and cooling systems, roof shapes, insulation and the size and type of foundation he plans to use. I will never forget the pool a friend of ours had built on her property in Rockland County. The man who designed it was a West Coast specialist, and that first summer it looked lovely, especially when the landscaping and the brick wall that framed it were finished. But when New York's winter weather got to those California materials, they literally crumbled. By the time it was rebuilt (which, incidentally, involved removing part of the new brick wall to make way for construction equipment), thousands of dollars and all sorts of time had been wasted.

It was late June when I asked John if he would like to design our house, and from the first he seemed as excited about the project as we were. But, he was careful to remind me, I would have to work very hard, too. That was music to my ears. I was much too involved to be satisfied with expressing a few desires and then retiring until it was time to pay the bills. Of course we would depend on him, as our architect, for basic and, we hoped, brilliant solutions to our problems and our needs. But on a non-professional level, especially when it came to the house's day-to-day operation, I wanted to help and be part of the house from the start.

But first we needed the land. And suddenly we found it through the same broker who had been showing us acreage since the beginning. He learned that Margot and Roy Larsen, who are old friends of his and of ours, were willing to sell some of their property in Fairfield County. Again we were terribly lucky. Unlike a wealthy friend who says, "I always buy to the horizon," we would have only ten acres of farmland protected on one side by a wildlife preserve which would remain leafy and undeveloped forever. We would have our privacy, and we would have our trees—among them some beautiful old oaks. Quite aside from questions of cost, they were important to us since really big trees are impossible to move and young ones require so much time and tending before they reach their full growth and good looks. What's more, it was comparatively high ground. Though only four miles from Rockmeadow, which was sixty-five feet above sea level, this land was three hundred and fifty feet up; while that wouldn't produce a panorama, we hoped it might mean that the way could be cleared for a very pleasant view.

As though all this were not enough, there were practical assets, too. There were city water and the electric lines that carried power to the Larsens. Neighbors on the other side were using city gas, which meant that it could easily be piped in for our cooking, heating and air-conditioning. And since this was farmland (it was actually three meadows divided by trees and stone fences), the ground was already cleared, which would simplify the grading problems considerably.

From first look, I thought it was wonderful. Even Dick had to admit that this land had possibilities. But before we made any decision, both of us felt John Stonehill should see it.

Only an architect can tell you whether the house you hope for will actually fit the property you've found or just what will work and what won't. He will know, for example, where the house should be placed. He may warn you before you sign expensive papers that the view you've set your heart on is a basically western one, which means that to turn your living room toward it would involve suffering the strongest sun of a hot summer afternoon. Or he may tell you, as John and Oliver told us that warm Friday in July, that the property was very nearly perfect. In fact, they said, it was so shaped that the house could be turned in almost any direction to take advantage of the prevailing breeze and the best possible exposure without sacrificing the view.

The Landscape Architect

Before we signed those final papers, there was one more opinion I felt we should have. It was that of Miss Alice Orme Smith, the most gifted landscape architect I've ever known. She has done any number of impressive things, going back to the days when, in association with Mrs. Max Farrand, she helped to design the gardens at Dumbarton Oaks. She also did the landscaping for Connecticut's Stratford Theatre as well as a most enchanting pool setting for the theatre's founder, Lawrence Langner. She had done all the beautiful landscaping at Rockmeadow, and I especially like the way she works. She told us it would indeed be possible to "slip" the house in among some particularly lovely trees just as we had hoped. What's more, she said, she could tell that we had good topsoil because the meadow grass was so healthy. (And so, I noted, was the poison ivy.) Her crystal ball doesn't seem to lie to her, ever. So when she said she could see beautiful possibilities in this land, we needed no further word. We decided to buy.

The Contractor

Before building could begin, we needed the promise of one more helping hand—a contractor's. As a rule, the architect completes his specifications and lets them out for bids before a builder is chosen for a job. With all the subcontracting estimates involved, it's a process that takes months and months; and had we had to live through it, we would not have had the remotest chance of getting into our new house the following year. But again we were terribly lucky. We already knew Mike Sochacki. He had been recommended to us by friends for whom he had built a house. Because they had complete faith in him, we had used him to remodel my bathroom at Rockmeadow, and he had done an outstanding job for us. I arranged for John and Oliver to meet him, and with their approval I took Mike to see the land. He was just as enthusiastic about the site as the others had been, and to help us, he agreed to do a most unusual thing: he would start his building from drawings before final specifications were done. That way he could take advantage of warm fall weather; and if, he said, he could get the foundation in before frost, we would have a house to move into the next summer.

For Dick, this news brought the whole project to life. A great deal of that last Rockmeadow summer was spent in talk about the new house and all we wanted it to be. It helped ease what might have been a sad time. For that year fall came early with extraordinary weather that was sharp, cool and crystal clear—and Rockmeadow looked very beautiful. I knew I would always love it, but the thought of the new place brought a wonderful exhilaration. And the pleasure both of us took in looking forward saved a great deal of the pain we might have felt at leaving Rockmeadow behind.

CHAPTER TWO

Talk, Talk, Talk

ALL that summer the air was full of house talk. We talked to each other about all the things we wanted the new place to be. We talked to friends who had remodeled houses and other friends who had built them. We looked and listened, and as we gathered ideas and suggestions we liked, we'd talk to John and Oliver about them. In the midst of all these other conversations, I found I was doing considerable talking to myself.

I asked myself questions, wrote myself notes, made lists and lists of lists. Upstairs and down, indoors and out, at home and on visits to friends, wherever I went, a notebook and pencil went, too. And when I turned out the light, they were on the table by my bed in case thoughts should go bump in the night—which they often did.

Interior designers love to say, because it's true, that to decorate a room successfully, a woman must know herself. It's the same, only much more so, when you're building a house. You not only have to know yourself, but you have to express what you know to an architect.

Too often people rush into building before they are really aware of how they want to live. They begin by expecting too much; for, while a house can change your life, it cannot make one for you. All of the experience you have had in other people's houses is valuable, whether it's a house you own and try to change to meet your needs as we did with Rockmeadow or a house you rent for a short time to which you must adapt. It simply puts you that much ahead of the game when you come to the building stage. It enables you to be realistic. And it seems to me that realism should limit planning to the present and the foreseeable future. For while some adjustments and additions may be possible—even planned for—a house that is built with the expectation that it will expand and contract throughout the entire lifetime of a family can only be makeshift during every phase of its existence.

Shape and line and color preferences are important, but the essential self-knowledge when it comes to building has to do with the way you like your house to run. Enter here all the complexities of parties and cleaning problems, of storage and lighting and laundering and a thousand other necessary functions. They all have to be considered. And it's impossible to marshal thoughts in order of importance. As you watch, they go bounding wildly from bathroom to garage, from icemaker to clothes pole; all you can do is try to get them down. I found that, for me, it was not so much a process of learning about myself as it was of trying to remember and organize things I knew.

My great fear was that in all my careful note-taking and analysis, I'd forget something really major. Because I know that happens. There are three stories, perhaps apocryphal, about omissions in building theatres. When they built New York's Music Box Theatre, for example, it is said they forgot to plan for a Box Office (in our world, those two words are always capitalized); they ended by having to steal space from the lobby, which has been cramped ever since. And the legend goes that two Philadelphia theatres were built without any dressing rooms whatever. In one case the owners were lucky enough to be able to buy the building next door, which had been a stable, and to break through the wall and convert; however, the only solution for the other theatre was to tunnel under the alley to another building where dressing rooms were constructed—an arrangement guaranteed not to make actors' lives any easier.

In another case, off stage, a friend of ours who was re-doing her house removed an ugly Victorian staircase. Incredible as it may seem, it was not until the remodeling was almost completed that she and the architect realized they'd forgotten to replace it; the house was going to be beautiful upstairs and down, but you couldn't get there from here. At that late date, the only thing to do was drop in a stairwell wherever they could, and she has never been really happy with the result.

I hoped, and as I write this I'm still hoping, that we wouldn't forget anything basic in our plans (since there's to be only one floor, we have only one set of basement stairs to worry about), but you simply can't be sure. So I kept thinking and re-thinking and making endless notes.

Learning from Rockmeadow

Rockmeadow was the logical place to start. It was closest to our experience, and it was many things we loved. There was a great deal of beauty about it, and comfort. But while individual rooms were charming in themselves, they were put together in ways that complicated life unnecessarily. And although there were many things we wanted to repeat, there were also, as there are in all existing houses, any number of things we made do with—like the uninsulated "dressing room" space I could never dress in because it steamed in summer and congealed in winter. The basic areas were there (the living and dining rooms, the bedrooms, the service area, the outdoors) but all of them could have been simplified and connected with greater sense. The object was to sort out our favorite things and visualize, for the new house, ways of providing for them so that the house would work better. The more we looked, the more we saw.

We began with the number of floors. Instead of three, in the new house we would have one, which would mean no stairs to clean or climb carrying luggage or flowers or Thermos bottles or laundry. We did think it might be interesting to vary the level a few steps here and there. I wanted some high ceilings and tall doors because I think they add such a sense of space and elegance. Especially, I wanted a high, airy look in the living room and the feeling everywhere of a house flooded with light. And I wanted an entrance hall like Rockmeadow's, a room that would say, "Come in, we're glad you came" and not just a place to pass through.

Clarifying Our Needs

One of the things we loved best about Rockmeadow was the way the living room blended into the sun room and the feeling both gave you of being closely related to the outdoors. In the new living room we'd expand upon that feeling by having even more windows and larger ones, but with none of the tiny old-fashioned panes that were so much trouble to clean. And in decorating I would use the greens and yellows and whites I had used before.

As at Rockmeadow, there would be a special place for the piano in the living room because Dick likes to work there. Near the piano he likes to have a small table, a place for pencils and paper and a good over-the-shoulder light. But there would be changes, too. The living room would be larger, with space for a dining area—one that could be closed off while tables were being set and cleared. I wanted a wall of books because we had decided we didn't really need a separate library. To save waxing and work, we'd have tile floors which would be similar in design throughout the living area of the house for the sake of harmony. But I also wanted the room to have the beauty and warmth of wood. I pictured a pale honey-colored fruitwood paneling—not pickled or bleached, and not painted, because Rockmeadow had taught me how much washing, retouching and care painted woodwork requires. Besides, waxed wood has such a lovely glow. We'd use it for the bookcases, for a fireplace wall in which hi-fi and the television would be concealed and for a storage wall between the dining area and the pantry.

That storage wall would right another wrong I had always felt about Rockmeadow's living-dining arrangement. There was really no practical, graceful way to set out buffet service. The dining room was too small to allow people to move about and help themselves easily; and, while guests could be served on the terrace, it was so far from the kitchen that it was impossible to offer more than one course at a time there. So we missed out on one of the pleasantest kinds of informal entertaining.

In the new house this marvelous wall of mine would change all that. Hidden behind folding doors, there would be a long serving counter with built-in warming trays to keep platters and casseroles hot. It would be accessible from both the pantry and the living room. The surface would be made of the best-looking heat-proof, stain-proof, wet-proof material we could find. At each side there would be enough electric outlets for coffeepots, grills and such. And *inside* the wall there would be magnificent storage space, magnificently planned, to house all the paraphernalia a buffet needs. There would be two-way cupboards for china and glasses so they could be moved from the dishwasher into the cupboard on the pantry side, yet

And there was more labor to be saved. At Rockmeadow the croquet field had been kept green by pumping water from the pond through a maze of pipes and hoses which had to be laid out and taken up at each watering. Now I expected we would be able to plant permanent irrigating pipes underground. And, except for the croquet area, the land would be covered in meadow grass, allowed, in fact encouraged, to look informal.

We also decided on some kind of permanent driveway surface because the loose gravel at Rockmeadow took two days a week just to rake. And the blossoming apple trees that lined the roadway were beautiful, but a problem; they dropped fruit every fall—some of which made wonderful applesauce, but too many of which, not so beautiful, had to be gathered up and disposed of. For the new house, I thought of dogwood trees, which flower each spring and have bright red berries in the fall. For a long time I had liked the idea of planting two varieties alternating along the driveway so that we could have American dogwood blooming in May and the Chinese later, in June. It would double the pleasure for us and for arriving guests.

If things worked out as we hoped at the new house, weekend guests would drive up to a door quite close to their rooms so that carrying luggage would be little or no trouble. Otherwise, though perhaps a little smaller and more convenient from a service point of view, the guest rooms would be very much the same as they had been at Rockmeadow. There would, of course, be comfortable furniture, built-in bookcases (a few shelves to give a guest a choice of mystery stories, poetry, a recent novel, some humor or, for serious types, philosophy) plus storage space for clothes and luggage. I also made a mental note to arrange a place to store a couple of bed boards, since more and more people seem to feel they get the best rest on a mattress that's extra firm.

My room would be blue and white as it always is, and have a

fireplace. This time there would be a dressing room I could really use—with good ventilation, no climate problems and, in addition to marvelous drawer and hanging space, a long rod for airing clothes. The bathroom would be almost a duplicate of the delightful one Mike Sochacki had built for me a year before we sold Rockmeadow. (I say "almost" because in the new one I'd slant the washstand marble so that water would run toward the basin, and tip the tub slightly toward the drain end; and I'd exchange the handsome melon-shaped hardware I'd chosen before for the lever-type handles that are easier to get hold of with wet, soapy hands.)

Dick's bedroom, as before, would have space for reading and television-watching, a desk to work at, a bath and the most beautiful view we could arrange. It was possible we would decide to repeat the greens and golds of his bedroom at Rockmeadow; on the other hand, it seemed to me that he might enjoy a change.

To use the word enjoyment in connection with such everyday concerns as linen closets and cleaning equipment would, I'm sure, seem entirely inappropriate to a man. But I'm just as certain that any woman who has kept house will understand when I say that one of the real satisfactions about the new house was planning its backstage mechanics—unraveling traffic snarls, shortening carrying routes for groceries and laundry and cutting out some cleaning chores entirely. Doorknobs of pewter, ebony or brushed chrome would not need shining, and all the furniture brasses would be lacquered so they wouldn't require hand-polishing to keep them bright. Throughout the house, the first principle would be to try to locate storage space for supplies and tools as close as possible to the places where they would be used. Built into the sleeping area, for example, there would be a linen closet for Dick's room and mine and another for the guest bedrooms; there would also be space close by for storing cleaning materials so that polishes, dust cloths, mops and what-have-you wouldn't have to be lugged to and from a kitchen closet every morning; and there would be shelves in or near the bathroom to store extra necessities. In the powder room and pool dressing rooms, there would be cupboards and shelves for soap and extra towels and a supply of lendable bathing suits and caps. But the major part of this behind-the-scenes efficiency planning was focused on the service area and its center, the kitchen. Basically, this included the kitchen itself with a maids' sitting and dining area off to one side. (In my dreams of the occasional winter weekends we might spend at the house, this would be a comfortable place for Dick to sit while I cooked; I wouldn't need to be exiled every time I fixed dinner, as I had been at Rockmeadow.) Beyond the sitting area, which would be separated from the kitchen by a counter over which food could be passed, there would be two maids' rooms, a bath and closet space—including a place for the uniforms and coats of maids who might come in to help.

At this point I should explain that I have never planned to get along in this house without servants. Entertaining guests, not only for meals but for weekends, is so much a part of country living for Dick and me, and it is just too much work to attempt without extra hands. But (and this is a very large and important "but") we will need fewer people and they need not be highly trained or specialized. If I had ever been left literally help-less at Rockmeadow, I could not possibly have coped alone. At the new house, however, I know I could manage at least for a while. The arrangement of the rooms and the marvelous equipment will make for great flexibility. I will be more specific about how this will work after we have moved in.

The kitchen itself would be the most beautiful in the world in the sense that it would *work* with such utter perfection. The appliances would be marvels. There would be a big ice-cube-making refrigerator and—because I've never seen a combination big enough —a full-sized vertical freezer (the old sarcophagus-shaped one at Rockmeadow lived in the basement and was a tremendous nuisance).

I would have my favorite gas surface burners (you can regulate their heat so much more accurately than you can that of even the most sophisticated electric models) and two of the miraculous new electric ovens that actually clean themselves. I wanted a ceramic-tile broiler—the kind that makes steaks and chicken taste as though they'd been done over charcoal. Margot Larsen had told me about some wonderful warming drawers she had discovered that really do keep hot foods crisp or moist, without cooking them any further, for up to six hours after they've been removed from the oven. Sunk in one of the counters there would be a motorized mixer base for snap-on attachments designed to beat, whip, chop, grind and handle every kind of time-consuming kitchen chore. There would be a chopping block, a marble-topped table, a small desk with a white blackboard above it and double sinks in both the kitchen and pantry, each with one deep side for washing big roasting pans. There would, of course, be dishwashers in the kitchen and in the pantry. I would store pots and pans in a large closet. And in addition to the pantry, near the kitchen there would be a larder (a walk-in closet with the kind of cool dry climate that's best not only for canned foods, but for storing onions, potatoes, fruits and even fresh eggs) and a wine closet that would also be uniformly cool.

I'd want a utility room with laundry equipment: a hamper, a washing machine, a dryer, drying racks and ironing boards; storage space for soaps and clothes-cleaning things and a comfortable well-lit spot for mending and sewing. At first I had thought the floor-waxer, vacuum and mops should have a home here, too; then I decided they would be handier in a closet of their own nearer the main part of the house. At the same time, I decided to stage a revival; I remembered an old-fashioned convenience with an ugly no-nonsense name. It's been years since "slop closets" (closets with deep tubs set at floor level to make wringing out mops and filling and emptying pails easier) were part of the best house plans. But, it seemed to me, they still made a good deal of sense because I have never liked rinsing floor mops in the kitchen sink.

We would have a back porch like the one at Rockmeadow and a double bedroom, bath and some sort of in-the-wall kitchen that Paul could use when the house was closed for the winter; but we wouldn't need the four-room caretaker's house we'd had before. There would be a drying yard in spite of the indoor dryer because laundry that's been hung out in a breeze smells so fresh and wonderful. We would need a rubbish-collecting area, parking space with a shaded spot so that guests' cars would stay cool in summer, and a three-car garage with direct access to the house. And that completed the list.

Although it's true that much of our thinking started with Rockmeadow, it certainly didn't stop there. It reached back to our earlier house on Black Rock Turnpike when I pictured guests arriving at the door and remembered how friendly and sheltering that clumsy-looking old *porte-cochère* had been in wet weather (in rain, snow or black of night, at Rockmeadow it was a twenty-five-foot open-field run from the driveway to the door). I made a note that there must be some modern way of achieving the same hospitable end, with perhaps a bit more grace. I also did a good deal of mental wandering through our New York apartment in search of ideas. From my closet, I'd adapt the design of a built-in bureau with both deep and the very shallow drawers that are so much better suited to gloves and belts and scarves. And I'd copy our liquor closet's combination of honey-combed wine storage space and shelves for the liquor bottles that can stand.

We remembered the best-loved houses we knew: Edna Ferber's Treasure Hill, with its lovely stone house, its magnificent view and its peaceful farmland; the house Lawrence and Armina Langner built for their son Philip, or so Armina thought when she started out. It was so simple really. There was this $100 barn she fell in love with and bought because it would be so nice to move it into the apple orchard on their ridge. It turned out that the orchard was rooted in a magnificent rock formation which made a good deal of expensive blasting necessary. But a fortune or so later, she did indeed have a delightful place—a composite of the old barn, which became a great lofted living room, and a lovely small house Armina designed and had attached to the barn's sheltered end. So successful, in fact, was the project that the senior Langners put their old house up for rent and moved in and Philip never did get to live there.

Tips from Other People

We also knew of two rather special houses on the shore: the Alex Lewyts' Sands Point place overlooking the water, which actually was a fascinating system of small contemporary houses linked by closed passageways; and the Leo Godowskys' on a point in Connecticut, with its Japanese-inspired lines, pebbled gardens and a swimming pool that is filled by the Sound. The house that was actually closest to what we hoped ours would be was the one Bobbsie and Gilbert Chapman had built high on a hill with a breathtaking view. All these added large and small ideas to our store. Each place, recalled or visited, was especially successful in the sense that it was so right for and so loved by its own family. And for just that reason, it followed that none was exactly right for us.

It was the same with the houses in the books on architecture for which I scoured the stores and libraries. There would be a wonderful floor in one picture (I was particularly taken with *comblanchien*, a light-beige French stone, and with the shapes of Spanish tiles), an interesting window treatment in another, a roof line or a series of terraces that we thought attractive in another—yet nowhere was there a whole house of which we could say, "There it is—that's what we want."

The story was repeated at the Museum of Modern Art's impressive exhibition of contemporary architecture—a beautifully designed show with a marvelous sense of dimension and space about it—but with very few residential buildings and only one that I found appealing. Strangely, I seemed to find all this more exciting than discouraging—it simply served to reinforce my feeling that the house in my head existed nowhere else; that if we were ever to live in it, we, with John and Oliver on the professional level, would have to create it ourselves. There was nothing I wanted to do more.

We talked to friends about the places they'd built and asked what they would do differently if they had a second chance. At first they were very protective about their houses; it was a little like asking them to list their children's faults. But after a decent pause, they all had suggestions to make. The Larsens, whose house was designed without a separate dining room, had discovered that their living room was really too small to serve both purposes (they've ended by using the library), and they'd also had to add screened outdoor sitting space. Both Captain Molyneux and Gilbert Chapman, whose houses could not be more different, felt they'd like higher living-room ceilings. Doris Vidor had used skylights everywhere—only to discover that in closets the strong California sun came beaming through to fade the shoulders of all her green and blue dresses. A young lawyer and his wife told us they had provided more built-in lighting than they needed in their new house (this is a thing that is actually quite difficult to know about in advance). They also wished they had added electric heaters to the regular bathroom heating.

In a long, thoughtful letter, Pat Knopf talked of the house he and Alice had built in Connecticut some years ago. If they were to do it all over again, they felt they might "do many things differently, but many of the changes we'd make would be because the children are older. A mother who wants to sleep near her youngest children won't want a bedroom wing far away, but when those children are older, she won't want them so near her." (The only solution I could see to that problem would be, in a house with both children's and guest rooms, to switch when the children are old enough—on the theory that guests are usually full-grown and presumably quiet.) The list of suggestions that followed were all very practical. Then he finished somewhat apologetically: "This sounds as though we hate our house, which we don't. We did cover many things in advance. . . ." Most of his suggestions were additions rather than basic changes, and I found we had provided for many of them in our own plans. Some of the systems he speaks of have been developed or much improved since he and Alice first built. Obviously, the heart of the house suits them perfectly. And they are now in the process of adding rooms that will give the children a nice buffered area of their own.

On the whole, it seemed to me that surprisingly few of our friends felt they would make major changes if they were to begin again. Construction problems, however, were another story entirely. Unless you've been through it yourself, you can't imagine the wicked gleam that comes into people's eyes when they hear you're planning to build. Even those for whom creating their own homes has been the happiest, most successful experience seem to delight in cataloguing the disasters they weathered. The implication, of course, is that you face the same, or worse. Some tales of absent-minded architects or collapsing walls or misdelivered materials were clearly calculated to terrify. Others were merely amusing: like Gilbert Chapman's account of their new bedroom thermostat with a clock that made such a racket they couldn't sleep. At considerable expense, they had it removed and replaced. And when the second edition proved just as noisy, they searched for the trouble elsewhere—only to find that the apparatus was set into a hollow wood-paneled wall which acted as a sound box to amplify the clock's workings. All it took to solve the problem was a bit of plastic insulation material.

In the midst of these friendly horror stories came a lovely warm note from Pauline Trigère saying that she couldn't bear the thought of our selling our beautiful house but adding, "I am so envious of the fun you'll have building a new one—planning, fighting, anticipating." And except for the "fighting" part, she was so right.

I had a glorious time. In architectural magazines I pored over ads and articles that told of miraculous new materials, some of which were already on the market. I dreamed spectacular dreams in which all these plus a whole new world of mechanical marvels were already built into the house. For example, one remarkable gadget I read about was said to whisk away the dust of a whole house at the flick of a switch; though I couldn't figure out exactly where the dust would be whisked *to*, I decided not to worry. We would certainly have to have that. There was also a system of vacuum ducts that eliminated dragging a clumsy cleaner around.

But the masterpiece was a scheme for a kitchen floor I dreamed up all by myself. It started off conventionally enough: I'd use one of the new no-wax vinyl coverings with a cushioned backing which would certainly be comforting to feet. (The new vogue for carpeting kitchens and bathrooms makes me very uneasy when I think of the inevitable spills of, say, a mixture of flour and raw egg.) But then my design took a new and different slant; I planned to have the whole floor slope almost imperceptibly from the outside edge toward a central drain so that a hose could be attached to faucets in the baseboard, and the whole area could be flushed clean in minutes. Then I had another vision—of a cook with very wet shoes or bare feet, and I abandoned the plan forthwith.

Visions of the fabrics, the colors, the flowers, the paintings we'd use danced continually in my head. There were all sorts of points to be checked. Since we would not have heavy draperies or carpets in the living room to deaden sound, I wanted to find out how effective acoustical plaster could be. It was important to keep the tone of the piano rich but not too lively. Dick had tried the piano in the Lewyts' Long Island living room, which also had tiled floors, and thought it sounded fine; so I would probably start my research with the sort of surface they had used.

There were questions and questions and questions—very few of which came with answers attached. Did we want an electronic garage door? Would we need snow-melters sunk in the driveway surface? Should we have a built-in fire-fighting sprinkler system or simply lots of individual extinguishers installed throughout the house? Would we need a household safe? (There hadn't been one at Rockmeadow.) And was there some sort of plastic finish that didn't give wood that nasty varnished look so I could consider having some wood floors? Should we have indoor planting? And was there, in Pat Knopf's words, "some easy sort of watering set-up" for it? Could we plant herbs between the flagstones of the terrace? And since the pool would be so close to the house, was there some way to keep the water in it warmed in winter so we wouldn't have to have logs floating on top to keep the pool from cracking?

One thought led to another; each question suggested more. And friends had suggestions, too. Jeremiah Goodman, the talented man who had done the drawings for *My Favorite Things*, suggested that we have the living-room draperies disappear at least partway into the walls at either side of the windows. That way, when the curtains were opened, they wouldn't cover such large areas of glass. I liked the idea, but I knew we'd have to wait and see if it could be worked out. Mike Sochacki told me that in some houses he had built he'd installed insecticide tanks in the basements and set outlets around outer walls so that a touch on a central button was enough to release a fifty-foot fog around the house that was death to flies and mosquitoes. Still, desirable as the immediate result was, it was the kind of thing I was really afraid to fool with—Rachel Carson's brilliant book *The Silent Spring* had made me extremely leery of anything that might put nature off balance.

Meanwhile, John and I got down to work in earnest. Armed with pencils and pads and lists and my scribbled notes, we began setting down on paper everything that seemed relevant to planning the house, from the linen closets to the croquet field. Generally, John's sheets were divided into four categories. First came "Adjacencies"—a rundown of rooms and areas to which any given space should be accessible—with comments about the function of each room. The combination living-dining room, for example, should be adjacent to the entrance hall, the pantry, the porch, the patio and the pool. The guest rooms should be near an outside entry, a bathroom and the linen area. So it went.

"Storage" was the next item, and here again lists were in order. The one for my room read: "Storage wall, well ventilated and lit; hanging space for clothes (blouses high, pants below; space for long dresses, etc.); portion of space with drawers; small closet near bathroom for bed jackets, dressing gowns, etc." In the last few miserable days I'd spent packing up at Rockmeadow, I had carefully measured every closet. Having these figures and knowing how well (or badly) each closet at Rockmeadow worked proved enormously helpful when we started on the new plans.

Under "Furniture" or "Equipment" came the lists of large and small items each area was to accommodate: some decorative (as "Table with mirror, bench and chairs" in the entrance hall); some as down-to-earth as "3 big bins, wooden counter, sink, shelves, pots, etc." in the potting shed. There followed a space for "Remarks" like "See Rockmeadow's set-up" or, on the pages headed "Kitchen," "Good direct ventilation for equipment, generally make all equipment white." In this department my favorite comment was John's, which came after a fairly complex set of requirements for the dining area: it said simply, "Dorothy, if we solve this one—*Voilà! Magnifique!*"

A page called "General Miscellaneous Notes," dedicated to bits and pieces like "Use aerators on all water taps" and "Find place for wine storage," took care of everything we hadn't been able to fit in anywhere else. And, with our lists of requirements all freshly typed, we were ready to get down to drawing floor plans.

As we worked, what pleased me most was that we all agreed completely on the approach. We wanted a house that would be contemporary in design in the sense that it would make use of all the amazing new materials and inventions available today. But we wanted it to be beautiful—not cold or antiseptic; a place where the things we have loved and collected over the years at Rockmeadow would be as much at home as we were.

To Dick and me, and to John, there was only one place to start: inside. We wanted to arrange the rooms so that they would work efficiently to make life as easy and comfortable and graceful as it could be. Though it baffled our friends, none of us ever asked what the outside was going to look like. We felt certain it would take its happiest form from the rooms inside. And sure enough, on my envelope backs and on John's masterful-looking drawings, both edited with Dick's comments—the house in my head began to take a shape of its own.

CHAPTER THREE

Giving It Architecture

WITH our impressive stack of requirement sheets to guide us, we settled down to what John called "giving the house architecture." It was a phrase that always reminded me that to him the word had a meaning different from the one most civilians give it. (For them, "architecture" is primarily exterior, a noun that suggests, immediately, adjectives like Colonial or Tudor—describing, as Mr. Webster put it, a certain period's "character or style of building.") Even "contemporary" has a few established connotations: shades of boxlike office buildings, glassy façades, concrete screens and roofs like aircraft-carrier decks.

To architects, architecture is something much more exciting. It means taking an idea of function and giving it physical reality. As John explains it, "It is the art of organizing the elements you perceive—surfaces, planes, interstices, edges, textures, colors—into sequences of significant spaces. That is the task, the ceremony of architecture." It is creating balance, pattern and order that satisfy not a pre-conceived form, but a pre-stated set of needs. It supplies definition (you say you want a large living room, but how large is large?) and detail (the hardware on a cupboard door, the brickwork around a fireplace). It works out the proportions, the ceiling heights, the sizes and shapes of doorways. It settles on materials and vistas, plots out points of view and exact exposures. Its aim is to provide a specific and beautiful answer to a particular set of problems.

Its solutions involve as many different approaches as there are architects to make them. There are still those, I suppose, who do begin with a pre-defined shape, as in Norman or Gothic or Georgian. Quite obviously there are others who, losing touch with the notion of flesh-and-blood people, strive only to achieve their notion of a beautiful shape. Their response to the challenge they see leads them off on all sorts of wildly unlivable tangents. I will never forget one friend of ours whose architect fell in love with a tree on the land where she and her husband intended to build. As far as the architect was concerned, nothing would do but that a glass-walled living room must be built around the oak tree. The roof would also be glass, the better to enjoy the tree's changes, season by season—elastic glass, of course, to allow the tree trunk to grow. What of the falling leaves? my friend wanted to know. Wouldn't they lie there moldering on the roof? And what about all those acorns popping on the panes? Simple, replied the architect, he would just build in water jets to wash them away. More running water, this time under the floor, would nourish the oak's mighty roots. Just this side of pneumonia and/or drowning, my friend finally put her foot down and located a new architect who liked people better than trees.

I remember seeing pictures not long ago of a house in California designed, down to the last footstool, by an architect commissioned to "do a showplace." The new owner, though by and large pleased with the result, admitted that his family had taken a bit of time to "fit themselves into it" and that there had been moments when they felt they ought to call the architect for permission to move a chair. I think that sort of thing is all wrong. I couldn't be happy with an architect who felt that only the furniture he designed and selected could properly be part of "his" houses. I think a house for real people must be flexible enough to accommodate the things that they, not their architects, love.

To me, a house is intensely personal as well as a machine for living. A public building is quite a different thing, impersonal by nature and definition, designed for use by many average rather than a few specific people. A house, on the other hand, can be successful only to the extent that it makes a particular family comfortable and happy by suiting their individual lives and tastes.

It follows that by far the most important step in building any house is learning what the people who will live in it really want. Surprisingly, this is something that most people do not know about themselves. And this is one reason, I think, for much dissatisfaction with completed houses. Needs must be clarified before planning can begin. Helping with this clarification is a basic part of the architect's job. This is where room-by-room lists of specifics can tell you so much and why making them *in detail* is so essential. As it is in inventing, recognizing the problem beforehand is more than half the battle.

Given these directions, it is up to the architect to take the problems and shape the kind of house he believes will solve them best. How well he does this is the mark of his creativity. Not only must he see that the house provides the number and types of rooms required, that it be as beautiful as possible, that the materials used suit the land and the climate, but all this must be accomplished within budget limits, be they small or large. With so many different goals, no wonder it is rare to find any single house in which they are all achieved. With such individual problems, there can be no inflexible rules. So it is quite possible—even probable—that another talented architect would develop a different but equally good solution. Architecture is a profession that requires custom tailoring to an exquisite degree. Nowhere else are art and science held down by so many practical considerations. No one expects a painting to hold up the wall it ornaments or a piece of sculpture to provide shelter from the rain. Architecture is the only art form of which we expect so much—that it be both beautiful and practical.

We had begun working with John and Oliver before we bought our new land and before Rockmeadow had actually been sold. John, as I have said, had known Rockmeadow since boyhood. But now with John and Oliver we went through it again, this time to learn from both the good and the bad things about it. Together we went to look at the Chapmans' house so that John and Oliver could see why we liked it so much.

There was a strong sense of understanding among the four of us, with each of us respecting the talents and feelings of the others and each making his individual kind of contribution. Like a good collaboration in the theatre, it felt right. And in spite of the dire warnings that continued to rain down, I *knew* the house was going to be not just good, but wonderful.

In the earliest stages, house talks almost always involved all four of us. But when our plans got to the drawing stage, it was difficult to rally all of us for every consultation. So a new system evolved. John and I formed the central conference team, meeting as often as we could—three or four times a week—to talk sizes, shapes, traffic patterns and materials. Then, armed with our conclusions, John would work with Oliver on making and modifying the basic drawing which they would then pass on to Dick and me for criticism and comment.

My architectural vocabulary broadened to include two terms that were everyday to John, but new to me: *parti* and *charette.* In the Beaux Arts days, the first—*parti*—referred to the student architect's original concept of his solution to a given problem. Before actually developing his idea, he was required to submit a sketch to the faculty. Once approved, this became the *parti* to which he had to adhere in preparing his final drawings. The word still refers to the basic general scheme of an architectural design. But with the founding, in 1919, of Germany's Bauhaus School, the word *parti* came to have a less limiting relation to the completed project. And this shift in emphasis (in which the final concept became more important than the simple presentation of an original idea) was the start of contemporary architecture.

Charette describes a process familiar to almost everyone who has to cope with deadlines. It is architectural slang for nonstop work under pressure. And it comes from the French word for "cart" because, in the eighteenth century, an architectural student's way of making use of every last minute on an assignment was to leap onto the cart that was carrying his drawings away to be judged and continue to work en route. That way he could add and correct right down to the final deadline. In a sense we were doing that, too —our pressure being the knowledge that unless Mike Sochacki could get the foundation in before the first frost, we wouldn't have our house ready the following summer.

Whenever there were changes to be made, they took time. But I kept reminding myself, at this stage changes were inexpensive; we were still in the sketching phase when—since we were not paying for the architect's services by the hour—it doesn't cost a thing to move a wall on paper. Once the house is actually being built, it is quite a different matter. Shifts are always enormously expensive to make when the foundation has been laid and the real walls are going up. Often at that stage alterations are impossible. Yet all the time we were building, friends would ask, "Do you find that when you get up to Connecticut you want to make a lot of changes?"

I never stopped being amazed at the number of people who seemed to take it for granted that this was part of the normal building to the land, insurance men and all the dozens of other people who process.

Each change requires an adjustment somewhere else. When, for example, I realized that soiled clothes should not have to be carried through the kitchen on their way to the laundry, we not only had to move the laundry and the hall, but change the location of the maids' rooms, the drying yard and the back door as well. At the same time, we had to remember not to let the back door get too far from the kitchen or the screened porch. Fortunately, all these changes were made on paper before the plans were set.

In the course of this adjustment process, John and I were constantly on the phone; and there were what seemed like hundreds of supplementary communications with Miss Smith about the land-scaping, Mike about his arrangements, lawyers about taking title handled this detail and that. The first step anyone ought to take in building a house is to buy stock in the telephone company. It should pay handsome dividends.

As we had agreed from the first, we started with the heart of the house—its function. Basically there were three areas to work out: the area for entertaining, which would consist of the living-dining room, the terraces and the pool (from the beginning, this was to be part of the house, not a separate entity); the sleeping area and the service section. Since ours was a one-floor plan, the most practical scheme from the point of view of both efficiency and privacy seemed to be to make a large living-dining room the center of things with a bedroom wing on one side and service rooms grouped on the other.

The living-dining room, the most important single room in the house, was, as John had predicted, not an easy one to deal with. The effect I wanted was that of one large airy room that could serve two purposes. Yet every idea we tried at first seemed to produce a floor plan that gave the effect of a dining room with one wall missing, which seemed rather silly. But after sketches and re-sketches, we devised a scheme that provided for my buffet counter in the living-room-pantry wall and for space just outside the pantry door that could be screened from view. A dining table or tables could be rolled into this area to be set or cleared without our having to give up the use of a major part of the room. In one of the early versions a long screened veranda with a dining area at one end ran along the back wall between the house and the pool. And then Bryant Conant, an associate of John's and Oliver's, came up with a brilliant suggestion to push the center section of the east wall out toward the pool. This gave the room a "thrust" section that not only provided space for a conversational seating group which was indoors yet dramatically near the pool, but at the same time served to divide the veranda into two separate outdoor screened areas—one for dining, one for sitting.

Having worked our way through L-shapes, alcoves and other variations, we plotted the surrounding territories: the pool and terraces on the "view" side of the house. The side nearest the road would have a hall that would serve both as an entrance and as a passage from the service side to the bedroom wing of the house; otherwise we would have had a laundry and cleaning parade running right through the living room.

Siting the House on the Land

Earlier, we had determined the approximate location and the most desirable exposures for the house; now we went to work to site it precisely on the land. Here, the most important considerations were privacy (the house should be back from the road and not too near neighbors), vistas (trees could be cut down to open views, and keeping the house high on the land would enhance them) and exposures. Originally we had thought of "slipping" the house into a line of trees that had once marked a boundary between two pastures. Then Miss Smith convinced us that although this would indeed give us ready-grown shade, it would be an extravagant waste of the very oaks and maples we had been so happy to find on the property. She suggested we move the house almost its full width north to a spot quite close to the edge of the property. It seemed at first like a rather strange solution. But there were only a few of the Larsens' work buildings near the line, including two red barns that we really liked. The service wing of the house, acting as a shield, would provide all the privacy we could want for the pool and the outdoor sitting areas.

In the course of our shiftings and turnings, we almost moved the whole house one more time to preserve an apple tree—one of three Miss Smith was especially anxious to save to shade the terrace. All of us agreed it was a beauty, but when I pictured it dropping fruit into the pool or onto the head of a lounging guest, some of its loveliness faded for me. In the end it was decided that since all the work going on around it would probably prove fatal to the tree anyway, moving the whole house to save it made very little sense. And with the advice and consent of Miss Smith, who felt we had picked the spot that would give us the best chance at a vista, the site was settled on once and for all.

At first we didn't agree on just which wing would be on which side of the house. To John, for whom each new day's sun is a joy, it seemed clear that the bedroom windows should face east. To me it was just as obvious that the bedroom windows should face south, since although both Dick and I are usually awake early, many of our guests like to stay behind shades till eleven o'clock or so. Nor did we want a living room facing west since, in our part of the country, western windows trap all the light and heat of a summer day.

Skylights in a One-Story House

The same sensitivity to light led me to veto John's skylights in the bedrooms and living room; but I loved the thought of using skylights elsewhere in the house. I think that one of the great delights of a house that is all on one floor, aside from the stair climbing it saves, is the way you can let light into it. I wanted to use daylight wherever possible: through windows in the living room, the bedrooms, the kitchen and maids' sitting room; through windows and skylights in the hallways; and through skylights in the pantry, dressing rooms and bathrooms where privacy ruled out the idea of windows.

At night, or whenever additional light was needed, four ordinary light bulbs set in the sides of each skylight, behind the frosted plastic, would provide artificial light from the same source that let in the daylight. In the living room, we planned on lights that would bathe the walls with a soft glow and, not incidentally, help anyone who might be hunting a book on the shelves. Impractically, I'd hoped that by using a similar scheme in the long bedroom hall we could eliminate the need for individual lights for paintings. Then John reminded me of something I should really have been able to figure out for myself (or, actually, remember since I'd had it explained to me quite patiently before), and that is that in order to "bathe" pictures on a wall, you must be able to set your light source far enough away to allow it to project at the proper angle. Otherwise, you end with a dim set of pictures surrounded by striking frame shadows. And even though our hall was to be a generous five and a half feet across, it wouldn't be wide enough. So we returned to the idea of old-fashioned picture lights—really very effective and not conspicuous when painted the same color as the wall. We tried to place the outlets where we knew we would hang a painting or an ornament so that the outlets would always be covered. As a kind of insurance, we decided to provide the same kind of outlets in the living room, just in case the planned lighting didn't do the paintings justice.

This unified scheme for general lighting would not only eliminate the need for expensive fixtures but would add, we hoped, an over-all sense of harmony. All artificial light in the house was, incidentally, to be incandescent because I think fluorescent bulbs bring out the worst in people and things. Since lighting requirements vary with occasions, seasons and moods, the whole system would be designed to operate on rheostats that make it possible to dial just the degree of brightness you want. You can't know, until you have actually lived in a house, exactly how much light you will need in each of its rooms. Without rheostats, you're committed to a fixed amount of light everytime you flick the switch. With them, you can adjust to any occasion, time of day or outside light. And should you ever decide to change your color scheme, you can correct the light accordingly. Rheostats also permit you to operate lights at less than full capacity, which greatly prolongs bulb life.

Plotting wiring and outlets takes long and meticulous figuring. We planned to use lamps because they can be beautiful in themselves and also because they give a cozy, efficient light exactly where it's needed. This led to further electrical discussion—some of it quite funny. We had planned to have the lamps work on circuits separate from the built-in lights. When we first talked the whole plan over, Dick suggested that in the living room we have lamps, hi-fi and television all linked to a single switch so that we would never forget to turn off the TV set or the record player when we went to bed.

It wasn't till several days later that we realized that if everything was linked to the same all-powerful source and you wanted to listen to a record or see a daytime TV program, you'd have to race around turning out lights before you could settle down. So the hi-fi and the TV set each got an outlet of its own.

We nearly made the same sort of mistake in my bedroom. In the course of our careful calculations, John paused to describe the way I would enter my room and, with the snap of a single switch, light both the bedside lamps and the soft lights over the bookcases. It was a pleasant picture. But its appeal lessened considerably when I imagined myself reading at night, getting drowsy and reaching up to turn out my lamps—only to realize that the other lights would still be on. To turn *them* out, I would have to get out of my nice warm bed and pad clear across the room. When I pointed this out to John, he looked stricken; then both of us started to laugh. We solved this problem as we did a number of others, with the help of an ingenious kind of outlet, one half of which is wired directly into the circuit while the other is connected to a switch. It gives you great flexibility.

In the electric department alone, there were so many things to remember. For safety and convenience, we thought it would be a good idea to have a switch near our beds to turn all the outside lights on and off. There were also the closet lights (the kind that go on when you open the door), the painting-light outlets, places to plug in shavers, clocks, radios and electric blankets, not to mention dozens of kitchen and laundry appliances or who-knows-what wonderful gadgets that may be marketed in the next few years.

In any future wiring or plumbing crisis, another great asset in our one-story house will be the "crawl space" under the house. It is floored with a thin layer of concrete—known, enchantingly, in the trade as a "rat slab"—which serves as a firm footing as well as a practical means of excluding the furry population. And when it comes time for additions, corrections or repairs to any of the house's mechanical systems, the crawl space (which is really high enough for a man to stand in) should prove invaluable. If, for instance, we should decide that we'd like to use a lamp in the middle of any room, no elaborate re-wiring would be required, and extra phones can be installed without damaging walls.

Obviously, adjustments are possible. But the incident of the bedroom lights serves as just one more illustration of a very basic truth: unless, in the process of planning, you actually visualize every step you'll take, you are bound to make mistakes. (Even with visualizing, you'll make mistakes—but fewer.)

From the start, I did considerable mental "walking" through the house. I'd be myself going down the hall, across the living room, through the pantry and on into the kitchen, where I'd sit down to do my meal planning. Or I'd be bringing in flowers and needing a place to arrange them. Next I'd be a delivery boy, staggering under a big box of groceries and looking for a place to put them down. Then I'd be the cook, rolling piecrust at the kitchen table. In this role I knew it was raining and the delivery boy's feet were muddy; I couldn't have him tracking up my floor or putting groceries down on top of my pastry. Clearly, there would have to be a counter near the back door, one not too far from the larder or the refrigerator or the storage space where cleaning things were kept.

I played so many parts that I began to feel like that protean actor George Spelvin. (Years ago, whenever an actor played two or more small parts, his own name was used only once and he was christened "George Spelvin" for his other appearances. I don't know whether or not there ever was a George Spelvin, but his name has probably appeared more often in programs than that of any other actor.)

At every turn, I'd try to catch myself doing something awkward or inconvenient. It was the only way I knew to track down errors in planning. And though I knew I'd never detect them all, my concentrated imagining did uncover quite a few.

There was the business of answering my bedroom phone. This episode always began with me in the tub, since that's where I usually am when the phone starts ringing. (I'd really wanted to have a phone in the bathroom, but John wouldn't let me; he says it's not safe.) So, grabbing a towel and dripping, I'd make my damp way through the dressing room, around the bed (which in my room diagram was placed opposite the fireplace) to the left side, where, because I am right-handed, I had put the phone. Mentally, I tripped any number of times and barked my shins on the bed; and by the time I picked up the receiver, I was always cross as well as chilly and out of breath. After several rehearsals of this scene, I realized that if I shifted my bed to the west wall, the phone (still on the bed's left) would be next to the dressing-room door and within much safer and easier reach. I made the diagram changes and sure enough —the next time the phone rang, I took my "walk" from the tub and didn't trip once.

Actually, the bedrooms presented very few problems. We planned on a room, dressing room and bath each for Dick and me plus a double guest room and a single guest room, each with a bath. The fact that this was one double guest room and considerable floor space smaller than Rockmeadow would simplify upkeep a great deal, but it did disturb several of our friends. Where, they wanted to know, would we put Mary and Hank, our daughter Linda and her husband, Danny, and our grandchildren? I am forced to admit, quite frankly, that we won't be able to put all of them up at the house at the same time. Everyone is agreed that from time to time when they do all come out together, it makes much more sense for them to have meals and games and swim with us; then we'll put them up at night in a very comfortable motel that's minutes away. Especially since Mary and Hank have bought a summer place of their own and Danny's work often takes him and Linda and Peter to the West Coast, it doesn't seem to us or to them to make sense to build in so much extra space only to have it empty most of the time.

In the bedroom section we had only one other major space problem: there was a brief moment when Dick's dressing room disappeared—or at least, became so small that John thought it would be better eliminated completely. He called me to ask if I thought Dick would mind dressing in his bedroom. I replied pretty emphatically that he would, since in a house with its bedrooms all on the ground floor, the same large, lovely windows that gave him his view would also rather effectively do away with the privacy needed for putting on clothes. Both of us like dressing rooms. There's something very nice about having a place where all your things are and you can air clothes or take them off without messing up your room. I don't need a great deal of space since I have drawers for underwear in my bathroom and do part of my dressing there; but Dick needs a place to empty his pockets, a mirror for tying his tie, a full-length mirror (I have a triple-mirror arrangement) and a chair to sit on while putting on socks and shoes. And it did seem ridiculous to set out to build an all-efficient house and end with an uncomfortable arrangement for its master.

So John obligingly said he would look for space. Since the house's general proportions were already pretty well set, it was literally a matter of finding, not making, room. And this is one of those places in which an architect's training and experience puts him so clearly ahead of laymen trying to cope with the same problems. I could see that by making the single guest room a bit smaller and by giving my dressing room sliding closet doors (so they wouldn't require so much opening space), we could loosen things up a good deal for Dick. It was John who knew and pointed out that on floor plans, where the scale is so greatly reduced compared to that of the actual house, the width of the pencil line that sketches a wall takes an inch or two off every room. And by giving Dick the benefit of several of these, we could actually add six inches or so to his dressing space.

In another instance, I realized that the twelve-inch-deep living-room bookcases on the plans would not hold some of the extra-large art books we had planned to keep there. Still it seemed to me as though I'd have to make do with their size, since moving that wall—even inches—would throw so many adjacent areas out of whack. John's answer to this one was ingeniously simple: he merely turned the studs in the wall that formed the back of the bookcase so that instead of twelve-inch shelves with a four-inch partition behind them, we would have fourteen-inch shelves and a wall two inches thick.

While I learned a good deal in this process of planning and re-planning, I knew then as I know now that there are certain areas that will, to me, always be a puzzlement. I will never understand the mysterious things that go on inside walls. The pure mechanics of pipes and wires and ducts, and the language that goes with them, are a foreign tongue which I'll never speak. All I want to know is that they work and won't cost the earth and won't need repairing too often.

I did try to inform myself. I struggled with the nine pages of suggested air-conditioning, sewage-disposal and heating systems submitted by the engineers who surveyed our "project." In the air-conditioning department alone, there were seven alternatives, and the first six didn't count since, after paragraphs full of incomprehensible terms like "ancillary" and "condenser" and "cooling tower," I'd be informed that this particular scheme would be wrong for us anyway. Pathetic and uncomprehending, I'd read that "This would require a very large and reliable well producing approximately 150 to 200 gallons of 53-to-55 degree well water per minute. The availability of such a well is rare." So, sadder but scarcely wiser, I'd read on.

One fact, translated by John, came out crystal clear: my dream of a dust-removal mechanism would add extra thousands of dollars to our costs; somehow, especially in a house that would be all air-conditioned anyhow, it didn't take long for us to decide that the old way would be the best way and perfectly adequate to any dust-control problems that might arise. The air-conditioning was to be zoned so that it could be regulated in each of the bedrooms; for, while I love it myself, we know many people who don't and prefer to have it turned way down or off. When we learned that water from the roof would be carried off through pipes that passed through interior walls rather than down the sides of the house, we did ask John to make sure to take the gurgle out of the drains. Otherwise, where air-conditioning, insulation, hot water and drainage were concerned, we gratefully accepted the fact that John knew best.

Having survived years of crackpot fire-extinguisher systems and exploding furnaces, I now have happy visions of no service calls for years. I may well be living in a fool's paradise. But in houses of a certain age, I'm sure much of the trouble can be traced to the fact that new systems have been superimposed on old. Even at Rockmeadow, which wasn't a very old house, wires and pipes had been so pushed, squeezed, shoved and coiled around each other that it was a nightmare to find a fuse or the right pipe in a bathroom. In the new house where everything has been planned for at the same time and designed to work together, I hope for years of peace. But we'll have to leave the details up to John.

Planning the Kitchen

There was, however, one department in which I felt that I qualified as an expert: the kitchen and service area. Here, as we had in designing other parts of the house, we began our plans with the measurements I'd taken at Rockmeadow. In this particular case, I wanted to duplicate them almost exactly because the kitchen there had always seemed just about perfect to me. Basically, it was almost square—about fourteen feet by fifteen feet—with lots of light and air, big enough to move around in easily, but not so large that it added steps to any job. I've always preferred its shape to those long skinny galleys that look so efficient, but aren't; there is simply no way to arrange things in one long line so that all sorts of extra steps aren't required just to get from one end to the other. Besides, narrow kitchens have no place for one piece of equipment I find absolutely essential: a marble-topped table I can get at from all sides when I'm rolling pastry or making a chocolate roll or even just sitting to shell peas (I hate to face a wall). There was just such a table in the middle of Rockmeadow's kitchen, which was an un-tricky, uncluttered room because, although I'm the world's easiest mark for clever new cooking gadgets, I don't like kitchens that look all gimmicked up. A good readable clock, a can opener, racks for dish towels, holders for paper ones and for rolls of waxed paper and foil —all these belong on kitchen walls because they are handiest there. But I'd rather have my pots and pans, including the copper ones that would have to be shined just for show if they hung on the wall, on shelves where they're easy to get at without having to play decoration. And because they're not always beautifully lined up, I like them out of sight behind doors that also provide protection from dust.

I don't care how good-looking a kitchen is, to me it is beautiful only if it is designed to work. Counters, sinks and appliances should be arranged around the walls in cooking-step sequence. Having space for cleaning vegetables next to the sink where the peels and scraps can be disposed of easily, having unobstructed counter space next to a refrigerator or an oven so things can be set down quickly, placing the dishwasher next to a sink—all these seemed so simple and logical that I always imagined there was no other way to do it. As it turned out, I was wrong.

I found it out some months later when we got to the point of actually choosing equipment. The fact that all Rockmeadow's appliances had been sold with the house left me free to start from zero on things that would work best for the new place. I suppose it makes me a skeptic, but I've never been able to buy the theory that because one maker's refrigerator is exactly the one we need, his range tops will also, necessarily, be just the ones for us. So I go down the line, model by model, brand by brand, for each item on the list. I'm convinced the effort eventually pays off in satisfaction, but it does mean more work at the start.

The ovens and broiler I chose were the electric kind that, when set to an extra-high temperature, will actually clean themselves. Another company made the two sets of gas surface burners I picked. The refrigerator had the same sort of automatic icemaker that for years had saved us the bother of filling trays and chopping out cubes. The vertical freezer we liked best for space and drawer arrangement was the same brand as the refrigerator. The dishwashers (being made today) are designed to hold more china and glassware, yet they take up no more floor space than the older models.

In some cases, the choice was made for us. Of several different kinds of ceramic broiler, only one seemed large enough to do meats for party-sized groups of people; only one company made the motor-driven "food center" I hoped would save so much time and handwork when it came to chopping, purěeing and mixing; and Margot Larsen had given me the manufacturer's name when she first told me about the warming drawers she'd found so wonderful. At first I had decided against installing sinks with garbage-disposer units; I worried about pollution and the things they might do to our overall sewage system; and besides, all the ones I had ever met seemed

All photographs by Ezra Stoller unless otherwise credited.

Preceding page: *Across the pool and into the house at sunset. The screened areas for sitting and dining are to the left and right of the "thrust" part of the living room.*

Following pages: *The front courtyard with the granite bollards. Service court to the left.*
(Photo by O. Philip Roedel)

The pool is enclosed on three sides by the wings of the house. This area makes a lovely sun trap in winter.
(Photo by O. Philip Roedel)

The green house faces the service area, which looks out on flowers all year round. The herb and flower garden is under the snow.

The "thrust" section of the living room. The painting by Zao Wou-ki hangs over the piece of furniture that houses the ice-maker and sink.

Informal Views of the House in Construction.
(Photo of Dick and Dorothy with Mike Sochacki by Ezra Stoller; photo of roof-tree party by Judith Stonehill; all others by Bill Maris)

The tablet set for lunch on the screened dining terrace. At night artificial light comes from the skylight. On the wall to the left is a bronze panel by Giacomo Manzu.

The entrance hall. The front doors were made in Spain in the 17th century. The rug and the two in the living room were made for this house in Madrid.

The television set is mounted on tracks and a turntable so that it can be enjoyed from any part of the living room.

The pantry lit by daylight from the skylights. The pass-through is on the right and the door leads to the screened dining area.

The view of the living room from the pantry side of the pass-through. The counter is set for a buffet.

A corner of the "thrust" part of the living room. The painting is by Graham Sutherland.

My desk space in the kitchen.

Dick and me with Mike Sochacki.

The bedroom hall with Mike's worktable in the foreground.

The swimming pool, with bedroom roofs and part of the main roof.

The stone wall going up to enclose the service court; garage is at right center.

The bedroom wing before the chimney for my fireplace went up.

The roof-tree party, June 1966: Roger being held by Jack, Mike Sochacki holding the tree, me, Paul Heetmann, Dick, Miss Smith, Oliver Lundquist, John Stonehill at extreme right and Ezra Stoller kneeling.

with a scribble of scamper patterns representing untold extra steps and wasted effort. The effect was that of a kitchen designed by someone who'd never tried to cook. In a way it reminded me of a famous house I've visited that has a "kitchen" in its living room. It looks rather like a large counter disguised as a counter. But when I asked its owner how well it worked, he admitted that he had bought a rather old-fashioned house a hundred yards away where all his food was cooked. It was then brought to the house by station wagon. (Presumably neither rain nor sleet nor hail nor black of night kept the soufflés from their appointed rounds.) He's happy with this arrangement, but I couldn't be.

The plans for the laundry were as inefficient as the kitchen plans had been. Being unfamiliar with the steps involved, the experts seemed to feel they'd achieved all that could be expected of them simply by collecting the relevant equipment in one room. Yet to any woman who has ever dealt with washing, drying and ironing, there's an obvious work-saving order. First should come tubs for soaking, then the washer, the dryer, the mangle, if you have one, and a place to iron. (We've always used an ironing table—a rather large one that stands at an easy height, about thirty-six inches, and is padded all over—for most delicate work and all the table linens.) Next come shelves for folded clean things and a hanging bar for finished clothes. In the new laundry, there will be a center for hanging, pressing and general upkeep on the other side of the room plus a sink for hand-washing small things, a hanging rod with a drain below it for drip-drying, an ironing board (with sleeve boards) for pressing, a comfortable chair with a good light for mending and a cabinet for storing soaps, dry-cleaning supplies, shoe-polishing equipment and that sort of thing.

None of this proved hard to adjust in the drawing stages, though it might have later when pipes and wires had been laid. When the drawings had been re-done, I showed them to Linda, who's almost as hipped on efficient kitchens as I am, for her suggestions as well as to Inez and our cook, and they approved. To me the changes were both a justification of my theory that a woman who runs a house knows best how to make it run smoothly for her, plus a kind of insurance that would help the new house run as effortlessly as it did in all my dreams. Well, *almost* all my dreams.

The house was so constantly in my thoughts that it even took over during sleep—an experience that I'm sure I share with everyone who has ever panicked in the midst of a large undertaking. There was one nightmare during which I fell asleep in my own bed in New York, then woke (I thought) in the new house. To my horror, I looked up and saw my door had a transom like those ugly little high windows they used to build over hotel and office doors. I went running—or, I should say, tripping, since the house was suddenly full of nonsensical little steps—through the house. Transoms were everywhere. Not only that, but the rooms were impossibly tiny. None of the furniture fitted; it was all stacked up in the middle and when I tried to straighten things out and push them back against the walls . . . well, there weren't any walls. Anyhow I found myself in the kitchen, and there, floundering about, up to her ankles in water that had collected on my glorious self-washing floor, was the cook, who seemed upset. I was trying to bail things out when, fortunately, I woke up, shaken, but secure in my apartment bed. There was no permanent damage, but obviously I had been right in my earlier decision to do without that inventive kitchen floor.

I didn't worry about John and the kitchen changes. His housekeeping experience, after all, is limited. And he assured me that the changes presented no problems. However, lest all this sound unbelievably Sunnybrook Farm, I should point out that we did have our differences from time to time. Being individuals, we were bound to. But we never really tripped over them, basically, I think, because both of us are perfectionists. And people thus afflicted (perhaps because they so often seem unreasonable to everybody else) have great empathy for each other.

It was tremendously difficult for us to hide our opinions from one another. Early in the game we discovered what John christened my "buzz words." It came about when we first discussed the roof. I was saying how beautiful I thought thatching could be, and John agreed. "But," he added with a certain wistfulness, "it's also a wonderful place for bugs to breed." That was enough for me. We scratched thatch from the list of possible materials, and "bugs" became the first of a list of words which had only to be murmured to deflect me from whatever course I happened to be on.

I found that John usually knew the minute I felt that something wasn't quite right. But I also learned that, almost without exception, he considered the likes and dislikes we expressed reason enough for change. As in the case of the bedroom skylights—which Dick and I deleted so we could escape the bright morning light John loves—this was true whether or not our tastes were ones he shared. He never made us feel that we were fussing, no matter how small the detail.

For his part, John was totally unable to pretend or make me believe that he liked something when he didn't. I realized that if he had been building a house for himself, he would have done things quite differently. Still I always had the feeling that he would never, could never, do anything in our house he felt was not basically right. Seldom have I felt he was trying to talk us into anything. In fact, there were times when he seemed to go out of his way to avoid influencing our decisions. There was, for instance, the day we discussed the fireplace. John suggested that the same small black bricks we were using for lining and facing should be extended to cover the entire chimney breast. They sounded exactly right, but just to make sure, I asked John if he would do a drawing for us. To my surprise, he refused. "It wouldn't be fair," he said. "I can draw anything so you'll love it. I'll make a small scale model for you. That way you can really see what it will look like." He made the model and we realized immediately how great it would be.

Choice of Materials

In John's book, the cardinal sin is what he terms "misuse of materials"—by which he means the use of any particular substance to do a job for which something else is clearly better suited. He is, for example, very much opposed to the use of vinyl in a bathroom to replace ceramic tile which, he feels, is far more easily maintained and more sanitary. It follows that he hates fakes, or *schwindles*, as he calls cheats in workmanship or material: plastic made to look like marble, vinyl flooring that mimics wood, anything designed to fool, to make you think it is something it is not. And I must say I agree with him. With all the hours and effort men have invested in inventing miracle materials that resist heat, dirt and other forms of destruction, it seems a shame that so little imagination has been used to develop, say, a good honest "vinyl" look. I can't believe it will ever really present its best face posing as marble or Delft tile or bits of stone forever imprisoned in jellied chicken consommé.

Any sort of dishonesty bothers John. I remember when we were considering woods for the living-room paneling. I had fallen in love with a Swiss pearwood veneer that John admitted was beautiful. But, he pointed out, you couldn't get solid pieces, and that would mean using some other wood stained to look like pear for the molding. Wouldn't it be better (i.e., more honest) to choose a maple that we could use all the way through?

John is one of those extraordinary people who really would like the inside of a wall to look just as handsome as the side the public sees. (For proof, see the fieldstone inside *and* outside the greenhouse.) And although that's the kind of dream I thoroughly understand (I like to make the lining as pretty as the dress) the practical me has to admit that it just can't always be done. To be fair, the practical John admits it, too. When we came to doors for the whole service area, for instance, John specified the paneled kind we were using throughout the rest of the house as a matter of course. Since paneled doors are expensive, and since the service area was to be distinctly separate from the other parts of the house, I felt we could economize, slightly, by using flush doors there; and John agreed.

There is, however, another door question that has, as I write this chapter, been left hanging. It's one case where John has very frankly tried to persuade me, and I have used every bit of logic I know to make him see the door (or rather, the lack of one) my way. The entrance hall has an opening at its left that leads to the service area and another one on the right leading to the living and bedroom areas. We agreed that the one on the left should have a door; and John thinks, for symmetry's sake, there should be a matching door on the right. I maintain that if there were a door on the right, we would always leave it open and ruin the symmetry anyway, so we really don't need one. At the present impasse, we've decided on a door frame, but nobody knows for sure whether there'll ever be a door in it. Meanwhile John smiles and refers to this as my "error"; he has complete faith that one day I will change my mind.

We will have to wait and see about one more of John's door theories. Plans for our "bathhouse" arrangement call for a shower with doors opening into each of two dressing rooms. Although John himself designed this (it really seems the best use of available space), he now sees it as a Mack Sennett setting for comic scenes of forgotten locks, impromptu invasions and assorted spontaneous meetings. Since we can't figure out any other way to organize dressing space near the pool, I guess we will just have to wait and hope for the best.

We seemed almost certain to disagree in the wall-covering department. I've always felt that patterned wallpapers add warmth and color—especially in bedrooms, where you aren't apt to have a great many pictures to hang. John, on the other hand, feels that this, if not actually dishonest, is a highly arbitrary way of imposing "just any" design. Obviously, if I wanted to use wallpapers, I could do it; but it was just as obvious that he would go on actively disapproving. For the sake of both decoration and maintenance, I was prepared to hold out. It was not till some time later when I started covering the market that I discovered a solution that both of us could live with.

As I've said, we never found John reluctant to make adjustments we asked for. Yet once I did find myself uneasy about requesting a change that both Dick and I felt was essential.

Designing a roof for a contemporary house is a special kind of business. Understandably, John wanted to do something original. His first suggestion had been that there should be one main roof which, starting from about eight and a half feet at the front door, would slope up to a height of, say, sixteen or eighteen feet at the back wall by the pool. I pictured myself in a slant-ceilinged living room, and it didn't feel graceful or beautiful or right for me or the furniture. So I vetoed that idea and John came up with a brilliant new thought: we would have not one roof, but several separate roofs, which would not only add variety of line, but would keep the house from looking top-heavy—a problem that often arises with one-story buildings. It would permit us to vary the heights of the rooms according to their size and to keep the bedroom-hall ceiling low enough so that people wouldn't feel they'd stepped into a chasm. Both of us felt that the outside and inside of a house should be in harmony. And since I much prefer flat ceilings to the pointed "cathedral" kind, I suggested some variation on a mansard shape. John liked the idea and went to work on it. His first drawings were elevations in which the roofs looked to me so exaggerated that they suggested chimneys on a factory. Although John himself felt that they looked "strong" and "romantic," he readily agreed to modify them. Dick saw the second version, in which they appeared to him to resemble ovens or kilns. Once again John went back to his drafting board to do a third set of drawings, which came close to what we'd had in mind.

All of us felt we were very near the point when we'd be able to say, "Okay, that's it—no more changes." We had settled on a "skin" for the house: it would be redwood, which not only weathers to a beautiful silver, but which, to termites and their various wood-chewing friends, has a repulsively acid taste. We would use the fieldstone native to the Connecticut soil for chimneys and low walls outlining the garden areas. And there would be lots of glass, especially in the living and dining area, to give that feeling of blending outdoors with in. The floor plans had stayed unchanged for two weeks; so, after agreeing to lower the roof lines once more, John went to work on a model of the house. When he called to say it was ready, we were terribly excited.

The Importance of a Model

Really, it was marvelous. There it sat in three, albeit small, dimensions (the scale was an eighth of an inch to a foot). Its H-shape was wonderfully graceful. The pool with its painted blue water looked just right. Under miniature trees on the bright green grass, there were tiny people strolling (this was to give us an idea of the actual scale of the house). And John had set the whole thing up on high stools so that it was at our eye level, and we looked not down on, but through its windows and doors.

We loved it, yet there was still something wrong about the roofs. I could see from Dick's expression that he felt it, too; and I was sure that neither of us was fooling John. I was worried because John is a creative person, and this was our first sustained criticism. I was terribly afraid that he might not see that we loved the house as a whole. It was only the roofs that bothered us, but they were so important they had to be right.

We had to tell John that to us they were still too massive. And he remained his usual, most understanding self. Evidently our genuine delight with the house had communicated itself to him. He said he'd re-do the roofs, and re-do them he did.

A few days later when we arrived at his office, John was armed with a new set of "hats" for our house and this time they were perfect. They had a kind of strength and the warm look of a French farmhouse; still the design was unmistakably contemporary. The contrasts—of dark grey slate against silvery grey walls, and of the smooth glass and rough fieldstone—was, in two words, simply beautiful. I could see espaliered trees against the walls. I pictured great pots of flowers, tubs of geraniums, hanging baskets of begonias and fuchsias. Suddenly, there it was: the house, very small, but very real.

The mechanical drawings were so beautifully done that I thought we might have them blown up and transferred to a vinylized paper and use them like wallpaper in the hall between the garage door and the service area. They would serve both as decoration and a guide for future service men who might be unfamiliar with the house.

Holding our breaths, we agreed: there would be no more changes. John could finish his drawings, and Mike and his crew could go to work on the foundation. Enthusiastic and happy, Dick and I left on a short trip to Europe.

Finding Things in Other Countries

I had planned to shop for the house as we went along—to investigate floorings and tiles in France and Spain, to order rugs in both Spain and Portugal. As almost always happens, we weren't able to do everything we had hoped, but we came away with some unexpected finds. As a matter of fact, our first "discovery" was something I'd been looking at most of my life. We spent our first few days at La Reserve in Beaulieu on the Côte d'Azur. It's an inn-like place, deservedly known for its comfort and its magnificent cuisine. We had been there before and loved it; it seemed an ideal place to relax and get used to the fact, as you somehow always have to, that we were really in Europe. On our first evening there, we wanted privacy while we dressed for dinner; so we rolled down the outside blinds. They were made of slatted wood, and they worked something like the top of a tambour desk. When not in use, they remained completely hidden on a roller built into the masonry wall above the window. To lower them you simply turned a crank and down they came in tracks set just outside the window. They were the sort you get so used to seeing in European hotels, apartments and private houses that you take them for granted. I noticed, however, that Dick was studying them with interest. "How would they be for the house?" he finally asked me. It was only then that I really saw what I'd been looking at. The construction of the blinds seemed uncomplicated enough; we couldn't discover any apparent reason why they wouldn't work as handily in the States although we had never seen them there. For our new house they would offer distinct advantages: not only did they operate simply, shut out light effectively and offer complete privacy, but when they were let down, they would serve very efficiently to close a house instantly without the time and trouble involved in boarding up. Unlike Venetian blinds, these are securely set so that they do not rattle, and being on the outside, they also protect the windows.

The next morning I went to the concierge, a gentleman as omniscient at La Reserve as his counterparts all over the Continent are, about what the French, with great logic, call "*les volets roulants*." Sure enough, he knew the name of the company that made them; fortunately for us, they had an office in Nice quite near Beaulieu. One afternoon we drove over and, *tout en français*, since there didn't appear to be anyone in the establishment even vaguely conversant with English, we investigated further. These blinds, we learned, could be made in plastic or wood, but the very best kind were made of wood imported—they told us proudly—from Oregon. (We later learned it was redwood.) They could be painted or stained. They could be made to operate by hand or electrically (at that point, my private dream was a combination of both); and certainly, they would work in cold climates—a great number had been sold in Scandinavia. Delighted, we asked the young man to forward catalogues and all relevant details to John at home, and we went away very pleased with ourselves.

When I wrote John about the roller blinds, I asked him about another thought I'd had. It had occurred to me that for the front entrance a pair of antique wooden doors—the tall paneled kind you see quite often abroad—might be extremely handsome for us; and they would be added insurance against that too all-new look contemporary houses sometimes have. John, who seems to be unfailingly receptive, was enthusiastic about both ideas; so we started our door hunt in the south of France and carried it on in both Barcelona and Madrid.

Actually, it was Dick who found just what we wanted in an antique shop that had been recommended by friends. I was laid up at the hotel, but he came back to report that he had found not one, but two sets that seemed to have the proportions we were looking for. I realized when I saw them a few days later that one pair would be exactly right; they were seventeenth-century with a lovely patina. Not only were they handsome as they stood, but they looked as though they could easily be put into working order; they were constructed in such a way that any necessary shortening (and it looked to me as though there would need to be some) would be a simple matter. A great antique picture frame, Venetian red and gold, also caught my eye because I thought it would be wonderful for the large mirror we needed. So we had both it and the doors shipped home.

With floor plans and color samples I had brought with me, we did manage to get to Madrid's Real Fabrica des Tapices, where we ordered three beautiful rugs for the entrance hall and living room. But our trip was cut short, and we had to forgo carpet-shopping in Portugal.

My other disappointment was that we were unable to find any sort of floor tiles abroad. While we were still on the Riviera, I had visited a factory that not only dealt in handmade terra-cotta and glazed ceramic tiles, but did some stone flooring as well. There was the *comblanchien* I loved so—but fabulously expensive even before you began to think of shipping. And having the tiles we liked made would take too long. It was another all-in-French discussion—delightful but unproductive. We looked again in Spain with no better luck. So, still floorless, we returned home.

With John, I went to a place in New York that we had been told "had everything." And indeed it did. There were glazed tiles, unglazed tiles, quarry tiles, terra-cotta tiles, flowered tiles, geometric tiles, tiles from Spain and Italy and France and even a few from this country. But the ones we liked best were from France, and even if they hadn't been enormously expensive, delivery dates on them were very vague—maybe nine months, maybe a year, which, of course, was too long to wait. Although the young men who owned the place were extremely eager to please us, they simply couldn't give us any guarantee. Instead of saying "yes" and crossing their fingers, they were entirely honest. While I was depressed at not finding anything, I was grateful for their integrity. At least we knew we had to go on looking.

I called the man in California who had supplied the handmade terra-cotta tile for the Lewyts' house and explained our problem to him. What we wanted was an off-white flooring without the reddish cast that unglazed terra cotta has. We wanted something completely stain-repelling and non-porous. Glazed tile is impractical for floors because the glaze will wear off in time, revealing a different color underneath. It also has a slippery look which, while it may not actually be slick underfoot, has a scary sort of psychological effect on people.

At last I found encouragement. Not only did this pleasant man assure me that his company had developed a glaze for terra cotta that was matte-finish, non-spotting and not at all slippery, but he told me about a new kind of tile in which he himself was interested. Instead of being ceramic, this was an epoxy tile—matte-finished and as strong as pottery would be, yet thinner and much lighter so that it did not require the heavy construction needed to support a terra-cotta floor. These tiles would also be less costly to ship. What's more, he said, whether I chose the terra-cotta or the synthetic, he could promise delivery in forty to fifty days once the order was in his hands. I chipped off a piece of some French stone that was just the color we wanted, and I airmailed it to him that evening.

When his samples arrived, I couldn't believe my eyes. The tiles did look just like stone. Their surfaces were dull and, because they were handmade, they had the same kind of slight variation in color I had liked so particularly in French tiles I had seen. They were relatively inexpensive. They would never need waxing; when I gave them the toughest stain test I know (crushing a wet teabag and letting it sit on a sample piece), all the liquid stayed on the surface. Later, I took a tissue and wiped it clean as could be; obviously this tile hadn't a pore to its face. With a classic pattern of squares framed by long hexagons (called pickets) that John had drawn in two scales (twelve by twelve inches for the living room, nine by nine for the entrance hall), we were in business.

We planned to use this miracle tile in patterns for the living-dining area and in plain squares for the bedrooms. In the bathrooms we'd use John's pet ceramic tile in off-white—but only for the floors and essential wall areas (around showers, for instance) since too much of it gives me a hospitalized feeling. For the kitchen and pantry, wherever people were going to be on their feet a lot, I planned to use a vinyl with a cushioned back that is less tiring to stand on than hard surfaces. However, since the choice of a specific pattern made no difference in construction requirements, we put off our final selection.

Somewhat belatedly, we decided on a surface for the living-roof buffet counter. John's original suggestion had been that we use the same sort of material that chemical laboratories use for their tabletops. Certainly its destruction quotient would be extremely low. But we discovered it could be bought only in smallish pieces, and what we wanted was a single sheet nine feet long and four feet wide. Clearly, we'd have to find something else. Our next thought was slate, which would have looked wonderful but is impractical because it is so easily scratched; besides, it must be oiled and constantly cared for. Marble, too, is troublesome where food stains are concerned, though we did plan to use it on counters in the bathroom. We considered black tile until I was told the matte-finish would stain; and the glazed version was too shiny. So finally we decided to use the same kind of tile as that on the floor, but this time in a charcoal color.

We also had to decide on paneling for the living room. From

the beginning, I had visualized a pale fruitwood, the color of honey and with no visible grain. Pattern in a veneer can be striking—as it is in zebrawood or satinwood. In one of the yards we visited during our search, I remember coming upon an extraordinary veneer panel which, had I not known it was a slice of wood, I would have sworn was a painting by Dubuffet. To me, it would have been too distracting in a room. I was looking for something quieter—a wood that would lend a faint sense of color and warmth without demanding attention.

I became fascinated with the variety to be found in those great sheets of veneer. Going through the panels, all numbered in sequence according to tree and cut, I realized what a tremendous difference in color and shading there can be from tree to tree within the same family. And as John and I covered the city from east to west, downtown to Bronx, I also discovered there were lots of things I couldn't have. There was no applewood. Pearwood, which has to be imported, was scarce, expensive and, as I've said before, not available in solid molding pieces. The walnuts, French and English, were too dark, and even the Italian, which was almost possible, was not quite light enough. I have never cared for oak used as wall paneling, but pecan rather appealed to me. In the end, however, a hard-grained American maple—one that could be stained the color I wanted, then given a wax-and-oil finish—seemed the most practical choice. Here, I speak for myself. At the end of all our wood shopping, John, who loves gleaming white walls, was still trying to convince me that we should give up my wood, wax and oil in favor of painted paneling. I came back with triple objections: first, that painted panels require lots of care; second, that cracks caused by normal expansion and contraction show up more in painted wood (an objection John said he could overcome with the proper kind of construction); and third, that the thought of so large a room painted snowy white left me cold. And in spite of the fact that John pointed out that painted paneling would be cheaper, I still wanted to try for the maple.

From John's point of view, simply because it was not a resource he had needed before, the residential hardware market was a brand-new world. Because door fittings seemed to present only reasonably straightforward choices, we postponed their selection and began with what I sensed might be a problem area: bathrooms. The handles and spigots supplied as standard equipment with most bathroom fixtures are usually useful and functional, but seldom very good-looking. What I hoped to find to replace them were pieces that worked as well but had more style. It had been a long time since I'd toured the bath-shop circuit, so I was as astounded and appalled as John with what we found. Such tortured shapes: swans spitting water and faucets that go leaping into space like Jacques d'Amboise. The soaring designs were outdistanced only by the prices. Bath hardware has grown up to be a gold-plated status symbol. Nothing you grip feels right to the shape of your hand. When I asked to see "something simpler," I was more often pitied than censured. And the less-than-rococo items we were shown occasionally were, almost without exception, badly executed copies of earlier good design.

When John had been stunned by the gaudier midtown outlets, I took him to a downtown firm I had dealt with for years. It's a company that has never let down its standards of quality, and it was there John learned that luxury hardware can be as beautiful as it is expensive; it was made almost like jewelry, and all of it was made to order. At one time or another, we had talked of using pewter, steel or brushed chrome. We settled on brushed chrome, which looks like pewter but comes closest to matching the color of the unconcealable plumbing in any bathroom. Remembering my experience with melon shapes, I chose simple lever-like sink and tub handles with harmonizing wall cabinets, towel bars, soap dishes and paper holders. At the same place, we picked door hardware and handles (also lever-shaped, also brushed chrome) for the main part of the house. With John's okay, I filled in pieces for the service area from a good commercial source. And when our Spanish doors arrived, John designed stainless-steel hardware for them which we asked the custom-order place to make up for us.

For the most part, the remaining outdoor decisions had to do with mechanics and were not awfully exciting. There were lightning rods, which John said we'd need, and a television antenna, which we hoped to get out of sight by installing it near the air-conditioning "tower." Miss Smith would make plans for the croquet-lawn sprinkler system, and John would make sure that there were outlets for watering hoses all around the house. We plotted the places where we would need outside lights, voted "yes" for a remote-control electronic garage-opening gadget and "no" on driveway snow-melters since we'd use the house so seldom in winter.

Landscape talk would come later, but John and I did make one more aesthetic decision in the outdoor department. It was one we were both very pleased with. Like all houses of frame construction, ours was to have a base of concrete blocks to protect it from the deterioration that takes place when wood touches or is buried in the ground. This not very handsome arrangement is often camouflaged with stone facing or tactful shrubbery. But John suggested a much more original scheme, and one that, to me, sounded perfect for our house. He proposed a sort of moat about two feet wide around the house to be filled not with water but with small smooth black stones. A few days after we had first discussed this plan, I was in a Japanese shop in New York and discovered that they had such stones. I was not about to order the lot then and there, but I thought I might take home a few just to make absolutely sure that John and I were talking about the same thing. They came in two sizes, but the ones I chose were about two inches in diameter and priced at two for 15 cents. I asked about quantity prices, and was told I could have fifteen pounds for only $9, bulk rate. Since the best available estimates set our needs at roughly twelve and a half tons, I found this figure depressing. Mike Sochacki came up with a price of $15 for sixty pounds, but that wasn't much better. John suggested an alternative: we could substitute hard coal (anthracite) at only $30 a ton. It was not a very appealing possibility. So I was overjoyed when John kept at it until he located a supplier who could ship all the stone we needed from the bed of a genuine Nipponese river at $150 a ton.

I was delighted not to have to give up my nice round stones. But I realized I couldn't always count on being that lucky. I knew that some things we had hoped for wouldn't work out. It was the law of averages. But I didn't go looking for trouble. There would have to be compromises; in fact, there had been some already.

Not that compromise always meant that we had to give up something. Our original roofing plans called for terra-cotta tiles painted an almost-black grey. Some time after we had decided upon them, however, I realized that although the texture and color effect would be stunning at first, as soon as those tiles began to chip (as they would, inevitably), brick-red flecks would appear. In the end, we substituted slate for tile and finished with a look we liked even better. It was also less expensive.

But my mind was already on other things. While Mike and his crew were excavating, I was busy planning the decorating. Compromises or no, I couldn't wait to get on with it.

CHAPTER FOUR

Going into Production

PUTTING it into theatrical terms, we went into production in the fall. The object of the exercise was, of course, an opening in summer 1966. And if the cast was to have a house to open in, that meant getting to work on two locations at once. Up in the country, they broke ground on November 1st, and Mike took over as producer-director, ordering and assembling materials (the architect decides what will be used where, but the contractor actually does the ordering) and assigning masons, plumbers, electricians and all the other subcontractors to their various roles. With the help of his draftsmen, John, author of the plans, went to work on the final set of drawings in which specifications were detailed down to the last keyhole.

I should point out that this was a unique way of working. Ordinarily, a contractor waits until all the drawings are complete. Then he lets out contracts for bids and picks his men for each job. It's a process that is safe and sane and sensible. But time was awfully important to us. If we were to make our target date, we had no time to spare. For that reason we were lucky to know Mike and to feel we could trust him entirely. Because he trusted us, too, he agreed to go ahead and start digging the foundation before all the final drawings were in his hands.

As interior designer, I did most of my work in New York, although the real decorating job had actually been started the month before when I *un*-decorated Rockmeadow. It was then that I had to decide what we would discard, because our new house would be smaller. I have friends who love to pack and move and start over in a new house, but that has never been my idea of fun. And loving Rockmeadow as we did, the prospect of dismantling it seemed especially sad.

It was not as though we were leaving all we loved behind. From the beginning, I planned to furnish the new house with pieces we had had all our married lives, things that had made us happy at Rockmeadow. I hoped they would look very much at home in their new places and dispel that cold, antiseptic feeling so many recently-built contemporary houses have. At the same time, I almost looked forward to doing some weeding out. In thirty-five years of marriage, you collect and become attached to a great many things. Some judicious paring would, I felt sure, help us start life in our new home with the most beautiful of them.

What to Keep, Repair or Discard

We had, of course, sold some furniture with the house. There was the curved sofa that had been made to fit the bay window in the living room and several upholstered pieces that went with the draperies. There were also curtains, carpeting and rugs which suited Rockmeadow perfectly, but would not have looked right in the new house. We also sold the round table in the dining room, the television set in its cabinet and the contents of one guest room because we would not need them.

There were a few pieces we would not be able to use that were beautiful enough to sell to an antique dealer—a faience font, for example, and the side chairs from the entrance hall. However, instead of trying to sell them, I sent them to a dealer who agreed to give me credit against other things we would need for the new house. It is an arrangement I have made before and one that seems to work well for both parties, since the dealer has more leeway and can usually give you more in terms of credit than he could if you asked for cash; it is similar to the advantage you gain by turning in a used car when you buy a new one.

Everything else in the house we would either take or get rid of—and that's where the work began. Our move was complicated by two special circumstances. The first was that when, years before, we went from Black Rock Turnpike to Rockmeadow, I had simply packed up and moved without discarding a thing. Attic stacks from the old house traveled almost intact to the new, where they were straightened from time to time and added to ever after. Now, with an attic-less house in our future, those mountains had to be leveled. The second problem was that we were moving not from house to house, but from house to warehouse, since our new place would not be ready until the following summer. If the furniture was to be ready to use by then, re-upholstering and repairs would have to be done in the interim. And everything had to be sorted and tagged with that in mind.

There were a few mementoes—mostly those connected with Dick's work—we felt we *should* save. Everything else had to be given to someone, or sold, or just thrown away. A decision had to be made about each and every piece, from the chest of drawers in the entrance hall to Linda's last doll and its wardrobe stowed in the attic. I put off the hideous business of packing as long as I could, not only because I knew it would be a great deal of work, but because I hated to have the house looking stripped and impersonal before we, and Dick especially, had actually finished our summer there. However, as Labor Day approached, I knew the time had come. Because the attic would be the most work and would be noticed least, I started at the top. It was the toughest, drabbest job I've ever done in my life.

I don't suppose there is a woman alive who isn't incredulous when faced with the contents of her own attic. On three different trips I had sorted through things with Dick and with Linda and Mary, deciding which of their possessions should be kept and which got rid of. Still, it seemed impossible that so much could have collected. The variety was dazzling. There were newspapers and books and musical scores (*The Chocolate Soldier*, *The Merry Widow*—all the ones Dick's family used to sing around the piano). There were teapots, wall decorations, lamps and costume sketches, a collection of stereopticon views of World War I and a dozen or so music boxes. On the sentimental side there was my wedding dress, bits of antique lace, my trousseau lingerie (all modishly long in back and short in front) and even leftover bits of our wedding cake. And in the exotic department, feathered division, I found egret and bird-of-paradise feathers (contraband now, but once my grandfather's quite respectable business) and the headdress, slightly molted, that Dick had worn when the Kiowa Indians made him one of the tribe.

All these treasures, and a great many more, were destined to fly off in different directions: my lingerie and the unsalable "hot feathers" went to the Metropolitan's Costume Institute; the Library of the Performing Arts got the scores and the music boxes. Brook Hersey was delighted with Linda's doll furniture; but the doll, a little affection-worn, joined the pile for the Goodwill Industries people, who do a wonderful job of repairing and distributing toys to children who have none. Porcelain went to the Thrift Shop, and we kept Dick's academic hoods and the war bonnet. I gave Peggy Weidman a bound volume of the short-lived New York newspaper *PM* because, as Elizabeth Payne, she had written for it—though why we had kept it in the first place, I can't imagine. And my wedding dress, which both Mary and Linda had worn, went to Mary for her girls.

As a matter of fact, a good deal went to Mary. She and Hank had just bought a summer place of their own in upstate New York, and they needed, as Mary said simply, "Everything." I was delighted because there were all sorts of things that I knew I would no longer be able to use—things that weren't especially valuable aesthetically or sentimentally, things that individually didn't even look very important, but that would have cost a lot of money bought new to outfit a house. There were blankets and pillows and kitchen things, books and lamps and ornaments, pictures and bits of china. There were daybeds, folding cots, a desk and a dressing table. All these big things, along with the provincial cupboard from the dining room and an enchanting little table Edna Ferber had given us, pieces Mary had always loved, would be sent by van. But that left a good deal to be transported by car.

By the Friday before Labor Day, I had sorted out the attic and the third floor. They were something of a mess when I finished, but I knew we wouldn't be using them. And I had the rest of the house looking its very best, just as though nothing was ever going to be moved. We spent that last lovely weekend with Edna Ferber as our only guest. And on Sunday Mary, Hank and the older children, Nina, Tod and Kim, drove out for the day in their station wagon. There was croquet, swimming, lunch and dinner, but in between there were literally scores of trips from the attic to the car. The parade was so continuous that Dick, who was sitting in the garden—near enough to observe the line of march, but out of trampling range—said that except for the fact that Mary, Hank and the kids weren't wearing black shawls, the whole scene made him feel like something out of *Zorba the Greek*.

That was our last weekend at Rockmeadow. Dick has not been back since. But I spent most of the next ten days there—tagging, sorting, measuring and packing for the move.

Packing, Storing, Moving Out

Moving out of a large house is trouble enough. But having to store so many things for an indefinite length of time presents very special problems. From the day it goes in until the day you take it out, furniture stored in a warehouse is all but inaccessible. "Dead," the storage men call it, and "dead" all our things would be to me during the winter months when I would be working on decorating plans for the new house. So before the vans swallowed so much as a very small footstool, I went to work with a tape measure. I took three-dimensional readings on all the pieces of furniture we'd be taking with us so that when the time came I could place them on scaled floor plans and know, with reasonable certainty, that when they were put there in real life, they would fit. When I'd made a list of pieces that would need re-upholstering, I asked my upholsterer to come by and make further measurements—this time to tell me just how much fabric it would take to re-cover each piece. Then I measured every bit of storage space in the house: closets and dressing rooms, all sorts of cupboards (bathroom, kitchen, pantry, miscellaneous) plus running feet of bookshelf space everywhere. That way, when John and I got to the point of allotting specific cupboard and shelf space in the new house, I'd have meaningful standards to go by. I would not only have a list of all the different sorts of storage area we would need, but, knowing where Rockmeadow allowances had been too large (my dressing room), too small (the pantry) or just right (the book department)—I could set aside less, more or the same amount of space.

These vital statistics went into a special notebook dedicated to essential decorating details. I made lists of furniture that needed repair or repainting, tables and chests with brasses to be lacquered, lamps whose shades would have to be replaced. And anything that needed any attention was marked with a red tag. The theory was that if I did this, everything that would have to come out of storage before the house was finished could be grouped in one place, and individual pieces would be easier to locate.

As I went over my lists one last time before committing the lot to the packers and movers, I noticed something interesting. Among all the things we had, most of them basically French Provincial in feeling, there was not a chair or table or chest that said "bedroom only" or "living room only." There was, for example, the hand-hooked rug I love that we had had made for the entrance hall at Rockmeadow; although its oval shape and its pattern might look attractive in the entry of the new house, it might also be right in one of the guest rooms. Adaptability like this would make my life a great deal easier in the months to come.

Quite proud of my highly organized state, I braced myself. To say I looked forward to the arrival of the warehouse men would not be in the least accurate. Recalling earlier moves I had somehow survived in spite of grubby boxes, great messy wardrobes and the rest of what I considered standard van equipment, I dreaded it as a distasteful but necessary evil. Years ago, you spent back-breaking hours piling your own things in trunks, smudging yourself with newspapers and inhaling the dust of a hundred other people's moves from barrels that really were barrels. I resigned myself to the same old horrors. Rarely have I been so happy to be wrong.

On the appointed day, a mammoth truck drew up and disgorged a uniformed crew. The cast was a classic trio: one three-hundred-pound mover who was, of course, called "Tiny"; Joe, the wiry talker, who managed to run through most of the R&H songbook in the course of a moving day; plus a third older man who steadily packed and packed and packed. As I watched these three begin Operation Transfer, all the dinginess I remembered seemed stone ages away.

They were armed with stacks of collapsed corrugated paper boxes, dozens of them in assorted appropriate sizes—small ones for heavy things like books and records, sheets and pillowcases; larger ones for bulky things that were not especially heavy (bath towels, for instance, and pillows and eiderdowns) plus great clean new wardrobes for clothes. For fragile things, crates were made; and for wrapping, there was newspaper without the ink and tarnish-proof tissue for silver. They referred to their boxes as "barrels" ("we've just always called them that"), but the resemblance to the moving days I had known ended there.

The system was very simple: I sorted, but they packed the fragile things. That way, they explained, the company was responsible for any damage that might occur. In spite of their obvious care and competence, however, I still felt as I always have: that it is essential to take out your own comprehensive insurance policy on furniture, paintings, mirrors, glassware, china—anything that might possibly be hurt in the course of a move. Good warehouses are covered for damage to walls, floors, trees, lawns, driveways and so on, as well as for the on-the-job injuries to the employees; but their coverage for breakage and scratches in transit is usually of the most superficial kind. In addition to the extra personal-liability coverage (if you are moving from one place to another, it should apply to both areas plus accidents in transit) and extended coverage on our property, I also had fire and theft insurance covering the time our things would be in storage—a not very costly extra in these days of good modern fireproof warehouses.

With our furniture gone, there were only a few details left to take care of. I couldn't bear to leave the house looking sad; so I had all the curtains laundered and asked our painter to come in and do some touching up. (At the same time he made samples for me of the living-room yellow and the blue from my bedroom, two colors I was particularly fond of and thought we might use in the new house.) I sold the little car we had used in the country, and the hi-fi man picked up the Rockmeadow equipment that would serve as a trade-in down payment on a sound system for the new house. With the new owner's permission, Paul Heetmann and I went through the garden for slips of flowers Dick and I especially liked; and for her I made a small collection of things she might find helpful, including the keys, boxes of Rockmeadow stationery and the die from which it was made, and a notebook with names and addresses of local markets and service people. At last, after one final thorough cleaning, the place looked as I had wanted it to—not as though it had just been vacated, but as though someone was about to move in. Then, finally, on the 15th of September, I, too, left Rockmeadow.

Excavating Begins

When, before leaving for Europe, we stopped by the site of the new house, a few trees and some brush had been cleared away and it was possible to imagine that a house might one day stand there. It was early November when we returned and, since I was ill and unable to go, Dick went up alone. He came home to report that a bulldozer had been in to open the driveway and that stakes marked the spot where the house would actually sit. All the dead trees and those which blocked Miss Smith's "vistas" were gone, and the views, he said, were beautiful. I could hardly wait to see it.

Late in November my moment came. And I must say that I was hardly prepared for what I saw when John and I turned in the drive that afternoon. The front meadow was solid cars, at least twenty of them, and it looked as though an enormous cocktail party was just hitting its stride. The excavation was all done, and in its depths, carpenters, masons, steel people, plumbers and electricians were all feverishly and concurrently at work. It was, as John pointed out, no mere coincidence. It was not only a remarkable sight, but quite unheard of and a great tribute to Mike Sochacki. It would have been a much more usual procedure for each union group to wait for the one before it to finish and move out before tackling its job. Somehow, magically, Mike had cajoled them all into working together, which would speed things up tremendously.

Every bit of it was exciting; the almost-complete foundation, the crawl space with its skeleton network of pipes, the grading that had not only deposited an impressive temporary "mountain" where the croquet field would be, but shaped the land so you really had the feeling that a house was on the rise. That was the day I met the beautiful golden retriever who lived somewhere in the neighborhood and had, it appeared, appointed himself house mascot. The men had christened him "Rodger," and he was both a noble and a sensible creature. We decided that he probably waited until his own household's children were off to school before he came to our house for coffee and doughnuts. He would greet the crew in general, make a trotting tour of inspection, then settle himself with great dignity near the one particular workman he had picked to belong to him. There in the cold semi-liquid clay he would stay—supervising, greeting all arrivals, yet never leaping, muddy-pawed, on anyone. At dusk when the crew left, he would lope home to take charge of his family again. (After we moved in, we learned that his name really was Roger, without a "d," and that his owners hadn't had to feed him all year. He had no children to watch over—he was a construction supervisor. After our house was finished, Roger went off to superintend the building of a church down the road.)

Dick and I drove up every weekend from then on ("Exciting!" says my diary. "Progress. . . . Exciting!"). But we left weekday supervision to Roger, and I went to work on the decorating in earnest. I was determined that the minute the house was finished, all its furniture would be ready to move in. And at this stage, time was particularly important. More than ever, it seems to me, decorating today takes time—not only looking for just what you want, but, having found it, ordering it and waiting for it to come. Looking toward that promised summer opening date, I had allowed myself months enough to find and order and wait for exactly the things I wanted for the new house without being forced to compromise in a rush to meet deadlines.

Since the Portuguese rugs I had set my heart on would probably take longest of all to come through, I started my shopping with them. Rugs for the front hall and living room were being made in Madrid; and there was the Rockmeadow entrance-hall rug to be used in one of the guest rooms. That left the other bedrooms and the sleeping-wing hall to be taken care of. I was lucky enough to be able to work out just the sort of designs I wanted at my favorite carpet house. Except in the bedroom hall, to give an over-all feeling of harmony, the backgrounds of the rugs would match the off-white color of the floor tiles that were being used throughout the house. But that didn't solve all the problems.

Actually, rugs in the colors I'd chosen—grey, black, red and white for Dick's room; blue, red and white for mine; stunning red-with-black carpet from Hong Kong for the hall—existed only in my mind. And although Dick knows immediately whether or not he likes anything he can really see, I know from experience that for him —as for most men—it is impossible to visualize a design in colors different from those he is looking at. He can't imagine a rug that is pink, green and white made up in grey, red and black. So because I really wanted his approval, I had the showroom samples photographed and we painted in the colors. Then, with completed "art" before him, Dick could *see* what I was planning and, since he liked what he saw, our floor coverings and our color schemes were set.

The living room would be wood tones and white and greens (from yellow-greens to olives—the color in the rugs we'd ordered in Spain) with some lively coral kind of red for accent. Dick's room was to be painted pale grey, with rug and fabrics of red, black and white; and mine, of course, would be blue and white with bits of the same red to link it to Dick's color scheme. The single guest room would be painted white or a tint of lime green with fabrics repeating the white, some greens and adding pink. And the double guest room would also have white walls; in it we would use the beds from Rockmeadow that were upholstered in mauve and let the rug pick up the mauve plus some shades of bronze and brown-green.

Of all the upholstered pieces we'd brought from Rockmeadow's living room, only one chair needed re-covering. The others, already done in shades of green, would work into my plan as they were. Garden furniture from Rockmeadow, which would be used on the porches, would be re-covered in greens to blend with both the living room and outdoors. Still, there were a number of pieces—a sofa, loveseats and chairs for the living room, for instance—that would have to be ordered and have fabrics chosen for them.

Starting on the Interiors

Once Christmas was out of the way, I started fabric shopping, which gave me exactly three days before Happy New Year and New York's now-famous transit strike. In the days that followed, I wore a footpath between our apartment and the new "D&D" (for Decoration and Design) Building on Third Avenue, where I covered every fabric and wall-covering showroom on each of its seventeen floors. I expanded my routes to include firms in other parts of town and new places I had heard were good. I discovered so many beautiful things that I kept having that lovely, greedy candy-store feeling—"I'd like that and that and that and a little of that." From each trip into the market, I'd trudge home with dozens of samples, coordinate them with the growing collection at home, set some aside to hold and others to return. Then I'd go to my graph-paper floor plan and visualize this pattern here, that texture there, shifting and eliminating further.

I've never tackled any decorating job without benefit of these special scale "maps" of mine. They help me "see" rooms taking shape before they exist in reality. Letting one quarter-inch equal a foot, I first trace the room's shape on graph paper, then cut bits of manila (it's easier to handle than paper) to represent furniture and label each one: "desk," "coffee table," etc. When they are placed on the floor plan, it becomes easy to see how successfully colors, patterns and shapes balance. Traffic lanes become clear, and you can tell at a glance whether a certain chair fits or there's room for a coffee table in front of a particular sofa. Kits made up for this purpose are available in stores, but the pieces are never the exact size of your own furniture; and since they end by being merely approximations, I prefer to make my own.

Never have my graph diagrams been more important to me than they were at this moment. I was trying something I'd never done before in all my years as a professional interior designer: decorating a house that wasn't there, placing furniture I couldn't see or touch (it was in the warehouse or at the upholsterer's or still lurking, undiscovered, in some shop) in rooms whose walls were still nonexistent. With my plans before me, I could picture myself in any room, sit in one chair, then another, look at things from all angles. Decisions were still difficult; the more interesting new things I found, the more ideas I wanted to try, but my diagrams made planning possible. Without them, I would have been lost.

Having time and the tools for visualizing proved a tremendous advantage. I was able to picture the things I had planned and to discard a number of ideas that seemed brilliant in the beginning but which would have been disastrous had they been carried out. There was, for example, the case of the living-room curtains. From the start, I had thought of them in terms of a marvelous big-scale pattern. Making a mental survey of the great expanse of window in the living room, I realized that large designs there would be much too distracting. In fact, the more I thought about the vast areas to be curtained throughout the house, the more certain I became that for the sake of a unified look from outside as well as for indoor serenity, they should all be treated in the same way. And I finally decided on the same kind of loosely-woven white linen I'd used in the sunroom at Rockmeadow. A soft, informal fabric, it would filter light pleasantly without demanding attention or pulling the eye away from other things in the room or the flowers, the pool or the view outdoors.

Because it was to be so large, the living room took the most careful forethought. With my manila pieces on the floor plan before me, I could see I would have to make changes in the furniture shapes I had planned to buy. The effect was too squared off. So I revised my ideas to vary lines, to include some rounds, some ovals and some curves among the rectangles. For instance, where I had placed the new round Spanish rug, I would replace straight loveseats with curved ones and have the glass-topped table cut in a congenial almost-oval shape.

Fabrics

Several times my floor plans saved me from really major mistakes. There was, for example, a point when I felt I had settled on perfect fabrics for every piece of furniture in the room. Then, with my samples and my diagram before me, I took one last careful mental stroll. Suddenly I realized how wrong I had almost been. For as I inspected and grouped individual fabrics, I could see that the things I had chosen were much too similar, all too damask-like in feeling, and, further, all of too much the same scale.

Since I had placed no final orders, I could still revise my plans. For some of the scrolled fabrics I substituted Thai silks—not the shiny kind, but with a textured linen look about them. One was a big plaid in wonderful shades of green; the other, a tweedy pale-green-and-white mixture. (Against this fabric, which would cover the big sofa, there would be lots of small pillows in all sorts of different colors.) I would keep the damask design in a printed Belgian linen (dark olive on natural) and use some chartreuse linen damask for a table skirt. A coral linen with a very small green figure would be added to cover three chairs, and in a spot near the door I'd cover a little square table with a particularly lovely piece of linen carpet—pile-less and not thick at all, and splashed with flowers in bright colors.

Again and again in selecting fabrics, I discovered that for this house I wanted neither the traditional things I had so often used before nor stark staring contemporary designs. Without being really conscious of doing it, I had drawn myself a neat new chalk-line between the two styles, and this was the path my choices invariably followed.

In the fabric and wall-covering markets, I was fascinated by and grateful for what seemed to me a growing trend toward special-order service. My peculiar difficulty in decorating has always been that I seem to want something unfashionable, something "nobody is using." (It seems flighty to me to approach decorating a room as though you were choosing a dress.) The winter before we started on the house, we decided to re-do our New York living room. I decided on grey, only to discover that grey, in all shades, was "out," and therefore virtually unobtainable in current decorating lines. In the old days, this would have meant End of Plans. However, today, if you can afford to be patient, you can have almost anything made. True, most sources that offer this sort of flexibility are available only through interior designers, and you need their expertise to make the best use of them. But nowadays at many places that specialize in custom orders you can have any print you like made up in precisely the colors you want on any fabric you choose—linen or silk or wool, cotton or synthetic. Best of all, it no longer costs extra (except in time) to have this done.

Having several months' waiting time, I took full advantage of these new privileges when ordering fabrics: the coral-background print for the living room (the sample had been black on white), the fabric for my bedroom (pale blue instead of yellow on white linen), the figured vinyl for the powder-room walls and so on through the house.

Furniture

However, when it came to shopping for furniture, I was not at all happy about the changes I found. I had always believed that it was pure extravagance to invest any but the smallest amounts of money in reproductions. All too often, designers feel they can "improve on" old designs by adding an extra curve here or more carving there—which only serves to destroy the original beauty. And good reproductions, while they may be quite lovely and serve you very well, are almost always costly. Besides, should you want to sell them, they are classed as secondhand furniture devalued by use—unlike antiques, whose value increases with age. So, when I discovered we would need some decorative pieces for the new house, I naturally went looking for old things. I stayed away from dealers who specialize in museum-quality pieces since I wasn't searching for period or signed furniture. All I wanted was charm and a bit of patina, the kind of glow that comes to furniture of a certain, well-cared-for age. What I found—or rather, what I didn't—was enough to make me eat my words.

So ugly were the things in the shops that nothing even tempted me. Never has such a thing happened to me before. Finally, with both my feet and my patience exhausted, I consulted a particularly sympathetic dealer whose shop has always offered some of the most enchanting pieces in New York. Having tried to find for himself the kind of thing I was looking for, he was all too well aware of the shortage. These days, he said, choice things appear in dealers' showrooms only when they are traded in or sold by private owners. And, as it happened, in the weeks that followed, a long (eight-foot-six from end to end) graceful sideboard I could use in the entrance hall did turn up in his shop thanks to just such a source.

But since coincidences could not be counted on, my dealer friend had an alternate suggestion. Why not look for old pieces of pleasing size, shape and design that, although in bad condition, could be made charming by a skillful paint job? Such pieces, he pointed out, would, in the end, cost no more than good reproductions. They would, however, have much more charm and would almost certainly increase in value with age. Remembering the secretary in my New York bedroom, I needed no convincing. I had found it in a Second Avenue shop in far from good condition. But its shape was pretty and, at the time, I knew a very talented young woman who did beautiful refinishing. After one trip to the Metropolitan Museum to see some painted furniture I liked, she produced a delightfully painted piece, one that hasn't been touched since and that I have enjoyed living with and looking at for over twenty years. So I went back to the search, kept my eyes open for pieces with painting possibilities, and found a provincial chest for the hall plus several attractive smaller things, all of which I felt could be refinished most effectively.

While still aware of the old things I hoped to find (a desk for my room, for example), I knew there were certain new pieces that would have to be specially made because they not only didn't exist—they had never existed except in my head. I called on an antique dealer who has found many beautiful things for us in the past. Since he also does some decorating, he has his own workshop staffed by highly expert craftsmen. And he has access to the finest materials, the most beautiful woods and hardware.

The first thing I wanted, to go behind a long sofa facing the fireplace, was a table with provincial lines painted Venetian red. Its top was to provide not only a place for a pair of lamps and small pictures, but a recessed place into which flowerpots could be set (with an apron deep enough to hide their sides) and, below, a shelf for magazines. Small tables made to hold pots of plants were used in the eighteenth century, but I needed one that was long and narrow, with marble pieces to cover the openings when I had no plants to put in them. To go against a wall in another part of the room, I wanted a piece of furniture made of fruitwood to house an icemaker, a small sink, some glasses and bottles, similar to the low buffet from Rockmeadow that would go against an opposite wall. The antique dealer suggested using a lead top, and we added sliding trays for greater working surface. Just as the flowerpot space—filled with geraniums or begonias or even green plants and ferns—in the table would be simpler and less time-consuming to keep up than the same space devoted to cut-flower arrangements, so the icemaker and sink would save tiresome trips to the pantry whenever we served drinks in the living room or on the porch or terrace beyond.

After searching with no success for a simple Louis XVI dining table, I realized that if I did find it, it would be wildly expensive. So I asked the same man to make that and another table to match which would sit folded in half against a wall when not in use. (He had made a similar mate for our antique dining table in New York.) Each of the two would be large enough to seat six, giving us a total of twelve places for indoor meals. And that number could always be supplemented by card tables and the round tops I bought to fit them.

To replace things that had been left at Rockmeadow, I ordered upholstered pieces: a long sofa to sit in front of the fireplace, a small sofa to go at right angles to it, two comfortable chairs and a pair of armless curved loveseats to be grouped on the round rug from Spain in the "thrust" part of the living room. In addition I bought a few occasional wood pieces, a small upholstered chair and a loveseat that turns into a bed for the single guest room. As a kind of insurance, whenever I was having a fabric or wallpaper made, I would order a little more than was needed. We decided not to have any fabrics treated for soil resistance, because it seems to make cleaning more difficult, and in this air-conditioned country house away from city dirt, it really shouldn't be necessary.

With these things taken care of, I made a trip to the local warehouse to get the Rockmeadow pieces that needed re-covering. Knowing it was the time of year when workmen in decorators' shops were not frantically busy, I hoped to get everything done and returned to the warehouse before it was actually time to move. It would be much easier on the nerves than waiting until the last minute. Mary came along because there were some things in storage that she felt she could use in their house. I wish I could report that, thanks to my ingenious tagging system, all was in heavenly order when we arrived. But it wasn't. Tagged and untagged pieces were mixed with an abandon which may not have been reckless, but certainly was confusing. And to add suspense, our things were more or less equally distributed over two different storage floors. Thanks to lists and persistence, we managed to sort out most of the pieces we were after. However, it was something less than a triumph of efficiency. And besides, it was chattering cold in that unheated building.

The Roof Goes Up

By now it was March of 1966, and Saturday trips to the house were the rule. Each one was as exciting as a "next week" installment of the most fascinating serial I'm ever likely to have a part in. There was progress, and we have pictures to prove it—the first of Dick and me on the doorstep (no door) taken by John in January. There are later additions by Linda and Danny, who joined us on occasional tours of inspection. Tod, Nina and Kim came up with Dick and me one day, and Tod took some excellent pictures from the top of the great dirt mountain that had been piled up during the final excavation. The studs were up, and the roofs. The pool had been dug, and we could see where the windows would be. But the greater the progress, the harder we found it to wait for walls to appear.

We had already made two major purchases for them—one for inside, one for outside the house. The first was a painting we had fallen in love with back in early September. It is a very beautiful portrait Picasso painted of his wife Jacqueline in 1962. She was our Christmas gift to each other and the house, although we planned that she would, in fact, spend her winters with us in New York. Our December discovery was a bronze relief, a unique cast of Giacomo Manzu's 1960 design for a handle of one of the doors of St. Peter's basilica in Rome. To both of us, the patina of the sculpture seemed to offer the perfect contrast for the grey walls of the house. We decided to place it facing the pool in such a way that it could be seen from the living room and Dick could also enjoy it from his bedroom.

There were, of course, less spectacular items to think about—everything from paper-towel holders and can openers to lamps and fireplace tools. Having arranged to have all the brass-trimmed furniture sent off to have its hardware lacquered, I wanted to make sure no other accessories still presented polishing problems. I had found an antique steel fender and some old steel fire tools for the living room, so I sent the bronze andirons off to be plated to match. Along with them went the andirons and tools from my bedroom, two Cape Cod lighters and a pair of brass candlesticks I had discovered on a trip to Toronto with Dick. While he was busy with a show (the Lincoln Center revival of *Annie Get Your Gun* was trying out there), I had a good deal of browsing time to spend in museums and local antique shops. Made into lamps and equipped with tole shades, the brass candlesticks and a pewter pair that I found were certainly useful additions. In New York I had also bought a pair of handsome bronze columns ornamented with gilt detail; with the bronze areas plated in steel, they would look wonderful on the Venetian red table in the living room.

But my real Toronto find was an immense British Railway station lantern that seemed just the right scale to use on an outside wall of the garage to help light the driveway. I had it shipped to John's office for his okay, and the look on his face when he saw it was something to remember. His eyes went right to some fancy copperwork on top; it was clear that he (a) didn't like it and (b) didn't think it would ever come off. However, when he saw it several weeks later with its gingerbread removed, he agreed that it was perfect for the spot.

Though the building was moving along at what seemed to be a very respectable pace (they were starting to shingle the roofs, and some of the redwood siding had been put up), John and I still had some material decisions to make. There were the floors in the service area to be considered. The most important area was the kitchen;

and that, for a while, gave us trouble. I had originally seen a new kind of cushioned vinyl that was delightful to walk on, but it came in such ugly colors and patterns that we couldn't bear to use it. I also wanted some sort of covering that wouldn't need waxing (not only does wax mean work, but it makes everyone nervous). Since, right or wrong, a dull floor, no matter how antiseptic in fact, never looks really clean to most people, I hoped to find a surface with a permanent gloss. At first John objected (the shine would be too distracting, hard on the eyes in a white kitchen, he said) but finally, with Oliver's help, I won him over and we agreed on a high-finish, but non-slippery, grey-and-white vinyl I had put in the maids' rooms in New York a few years earlier. But the pattern had been discontinued; so we started again. The more we looked, the surer we became that my pattern had been taken off the line because it was good-looking. Most of what we saw, especially all those designs that came sparked with gold and silver, was very depressing. We were just about to give up and willing to settle for gravel when John came up with something perfectly marvelous. It is vinyl with a slightly textured surface flecked in off-whites, and it is cushioned with a foam-rubber substance that makes it wonderfully resilient. What's more, it is guaranteed for five years against any sort of difficulty with installation or wear. We used it throughout the service area except for the bathrooms, the potting shed and the caretaker's galley. For these we picked a spattered grey-vinyl asbestos tile that wears very well, takes minimum care and is considerably less expensive than the cushioned vinyl. The only built-in color in the service area would be the lemon yellow of the Formica we chose for the wall space between the cabinets and the counter tops in the kitchen and the pantry.

I took John to meet my favorite marble man (who, when he's at work in his shop, always looks as though he's made of marble dust from head to toe), where we picked out the kinds of marble we wanted for the counters in our bathrooms, the guest bathrooms and the powder room. For the guest rooms and my bath we chose an almost-white grey with some veining. For Dick's room and the powder room, we decided on a darker grey veined with white. We would use one-inch white matte-finish ceramic tiles for wall areas around the tubs where they were needed, and for all the bathroom floors except mine which, because it is large, needs a larger-scale tile. But I vetoed John's suggestion that we tile all the walls to a height of three or four feet. To me it would have looked too clinical.

I did, however, come around to his way of thinking in one important instance: to have or not to have patterned wallpaper. It was charming in the halls and bedrooms at Rockmeadow, but I realized it would be out of place in the new house. Through the various stages of thinking and talking and planning, I had become increasingly aware that this house would have a quite different look from anything I had ever worked on before. Maybe as I've grown older, I've grown bolder. I wanted this house to have the warmth that Rockmeadow had had, but in its own special way. So I found myself choosing upholstery fabrics with stronger colors and picking figured rugs although the ones we'd had before had always been plain. Except for my bathroom and the powder room, where I still planned to use striped and figured vinyl coverings, I had come to agree with John that walls painted in white or pale colors would be more effective and would be in complete harmony with the white linen curtains throughout the front of the house. In the service area we would take advantage of the practicality and easy maintenance of a good-looking textured white vinyl.

Storage Space

One area in which John and I did a tremendous amount of work was storage space. Each section had to be detailed according to its use:

the living-room wall, within which card tables and tabletops were to be stored; the pantry, where adjustable shelves seemed to be the best solution to the problems presented by the miscellaneous sizes and shapes of trays, serving pieces, china and glasses (flatware would have its own cloth-lined drawers). We also planned ventilated space to store wines and a larder for perishable foods like fruits, vegetables and potatoes that are not at their best refrigerated. Canned goods and cleaning equipment would go into cabinets with adjustable shelves.

In the bedroom wing we mapped out Dick's and my dressing rooms (I needed considerably less space than I'd had at Rockmeadow, but he would have more), storage for linens and cleaning equipment in the bedroom hall and closets for the guest rooms. To simplify the arrangement of furniture in the guest rooms, we gave each closet a built-in chest of drawers as well as shoe shelves and hanging bars. From experience, I realized I would also need an out-of-season storage place for summer clothes and sports equipment in winter, and for winter clothes in summer (when the children were small, we needed space for skis and sleds, too). So we set aside an area under the only stairs in the house, those going down to the cellar, for this sort of "dead storage." Summer and winter bedding would alternate on shelves in the closets of rooms in which they would be used.

The floors of all the closets would be a good-looking neutral vinyl that goes particularly well with the California tile; and I discussed with John the idea of having wall vinyl applied to the shelves as it would simplify cleaning them.

Our most important decisions had to do with the ceiling heights in the living room, Dick's room, my room and the double guest room; all others were to be uniformly eight-foot-six-inches because small areas and long halls are unpleasant with high ceilings. Since it really is such a subjective matter and depends so much on the size of the rooms themselves, we felt the final decisions should be made on the site. The carpenters tacked up large pieces of plywood at various heights on some of the roof supports in the living room and in one of the bedrooms so that we could actually see how the ceilings would look. It turned out that the fourteen-foot-six height we had pictured for the high part of the living room would be perfect (the ceiling in the "thrust" area would be lower—only eight-foot-six); but the thirteen-foot ceilings in the bedrooms, which had bothered me on paper, gave us a sort of bottom-of-the-well feeling, and we decided to lower them to twelve-foot-six. Repeating the two levels of the living-room ceiling, Dick's room and mine would each have a cozy, lowered section—Dick's near the pool, mine near the fireplace.

The only major compromise up to this point involved the roller blinds that were to come from France. John told me that since our house was basically a wood-frame construction, the blinds could not be set flush with the outside walls as they are in Europe, where stone is the common building material and walls are considerably thicker. He also said that this sort of blind would not be practical for the larger windows in the living room. I didn't mind about the living-room windows since we would want to black them out completely only during the winter months when the house would be closed. But John's plan to hide the roller mechanisms in a sort of eyebrow box over each window worried me. I didn't see how they could help but look "tacked on," and I was frankly very skeptical when John said he could show me, by revising the model of the house, that they would really be entirely presentable. As it turned out, he was righter than either of us had thought he would be—the "eyebrows" actually improved the looks of the house by adding interest to the fascia. We were all terribly pleased, and the blinds were ordered.

Without any conscious effort on our part, we seemed to have planned quite an international house. There were the blinds from France, the doors from Madrid, the Manzu from Rome, the rugs from Spain and Portugal and Hong Kong. The redwood (from California, like the floor tiles) would be roofed with slate from Vermont, moated by pebbles from Japan and serve as background for the British lantern. Yet, varied as their homelands were, it seemed to us these things would all blend beautifully.

There were still all sorts of small items to take care of, such as sunken places for doormats and a spot for a television set in my bedroom (taking a cue from Kitty Hart, I would hide it beneath the skirt of a small round table). We picked mesh-curtain screens for the fireplaces and the hardware for the front doors. I had a good deal of trouble convincing the hi-fi engineer who came to discuss plans that we didn't want all the bedrooms wired for sound. Since for Dick, music is something to concentrate on—never just background—we don't want music wherever we go. The poor man was disappointed, but he agreed to limit the system to the living room.

Gradually, everything was falling into place. Now that the furniture, rugs and fabrics had all been ordered, I had a beautiful dream of three lovely months when there would be almost nothing to do and I wouldn't have to run as much or as fast as I had. John and I went over our "specifics" sheets once more and were surprised to discover that our original plans had been changed so little. The only revision that stands out in my mind is the relatively minor matter of the steps between rooms, which were eliminated in the final plans, not only because they were troublesome, but because the variation in ceiling heights made them visually unnecessary.

At this point, although you could still see through its "walls," the house itself began to seem very real. There it stood on the highest point of the property; we could see that the views were very beautiful. The house seemed almost to be floating—it was so airy and full of light. The bedrooms looked smaller than they would eventually (all rooms do without furniture). The living room looked big, though not so frightening in its proportions as I later discovered it had seemed to others. But the kitchen really startled me; it looked simply immense until I adjusted to the notion that cabinets and appliances would trim it by two feet all around the walls and that this was really two rooms anyway: a kitchen and a sitting room divided by a counter.

While there would still be details to attend to, all the things I was sure we would need had finally been taken care of. It had been a lot of work, and time-consuming, but all intensely pleasurable. Then suddenly, with so many of the problems sorted out, I began to feel terribly impatient. The rooms seemed to have come together beautifully, but I wanted to *see* how they looked. I could hardly wait to move in, to unpack, to stock the cupboards and set our books on the shelves that weren't yet there. Since that was impossible, I tried the next best thing: I consoled myself with the thought that summer and our promised moving day were only a few months away.

CHAPTER FIVE

The Price of a Dream

MY first inkling that something was wrong came that Thursday when John called. The drawings, he said, were complete, and we would at last be able to get exact costs on all the mechanical systems. In fact, he had the final figures for electrical installations in his hand. Pause. They were pretty staggering, he said. We both paused, then he quoted a figure. He was right: I was staggered. I made a little joke: we could light the house with candles, I said. No, that would be too expensive. Maybe kerosene. . . . It was a very little joke. And it was a very serious situation.

I would really rather not talk about money. We have all been taught it isn't quite nice to. And since money means so many different things and feelings about it are so highly personal, it is a subject about which it is very easy to be misunderstood. Yet when it comes to building—or even remodeling—cost is such a vitally important factor that it simply would not be fair for me to avoid it here. I'm going to be completely honest about the problems, but I'm not going to give any figures.

A few days later John brought us all the final ghastly statistics. In terms of what we had planned to spend, they were appalling. I felt guilty, abject, apologetic and literally ill.

From the beginning, I want to be quite clear about one point: none of our money problems arose from our having been foolish or taken for suckers; no one took advantage of us. Mike was everything we had hoped he would be. And from start to finish, with one exception which I will go into later, the men who worked on the house were a remarkably fine crew—not only skilled, but cooperative and pleasant to be around. We had not been negligent, or careless, or outrageously extravagant in our decisions. And because we knew it would increase costs enormously, we had made no changes in the plans once the work on the foundation was under way. Our troubles stemmed from entirely different sources.

First, and most obvious now: we had set ourselves up for a shock. Because it was so personally important to us to have a house for the very next summer, we had gone ahead, broken ground and started before any estimates were in. Had we waited for completed specifications, we would, of course, have had in advance a much more accurate idea of what costs would be. On the other hand, because costs of material and labor were steadily rising, the totals would have been even higher had we waited to get all the estimates. As the saying goes, had we known then what we know now, there might very well have been no house at all.

Second, there is absolutely nothing economical about building a one-story house, except the remote possibility that, in the dim future, having no stairs might save doctors' bills by preventing wear on the heart. It takes miles more of everything: pipes, wires, ducts, telephone lines, heating systems—all those highly mechanical, between-the-walls things about which I am so vague. And more miles means more work, more time, more labor and higher installation costs.

And third, everyone wanted the best for us. John and I had recognized each other from the beginning for the perfectionists we are. But we weren't the only ones. Early in the planning, John had decided to employ a firm of highly competent engineers to design the mechanical systems for the house. The plans they had come up with were beautiful, highly sophisticated and, therefore, incredibly expensive.

But several things had lulled me into thinking that throughout the planning and from the start of actual building, costs *were* being kept in line. The brand of perfectionism of which John and I are victims insists on integrity of material and design—on building the best way. We made choices on the basis of both aesthetics and function. But that can mean savings as well as extra expense. It already had.

To achieve a sense of unity and serenity, we had used as few different kinds of material as possible throughout the house; and quantity ordering should have helped to keep costs down. Because brick would have been too formal in feeling for the kind of house we wanted, we had chosen instead to use wood, which was certainly less expensive. Because of the chipping problem inherent in painted roof tiles, we had substituted Vermont slate which was, again, less costly. And I remember when we decided that the California floor tile had the color, the texture, the stain-resistance, all the qualities we had hoped to find, John told me there was a bonus involved: its light weight compared to ceramic tile would mean substantial savings on heavy support construction.

We had also done what I fondly thought was some economizing. Extravagances like the humidifier and the dust-remover—unnecessary dreams, really—had been eliminated early in our calculations. Because we felt we wouldn't be using the house in the wintertime, we decided against having a snow-melting system built into the driveway. My inventive kitchen floor had disappeared, and so had the central vacuum cleaner when I realized that we just didn't need it for the floors and rugs we were using. And when I discovered that that little flower-conditioning refrigerator would cost an absurd $2,500, nobody had had to tell me to write it out, too.

Everyone had told us the house would cost more than we thought, yet I found myself totally unprepared for the enormity of it all. In a sense, it was my own fault. I had bolstered myself with the same silly rationalizations that everybody uses. There was the classic trap: how can you skimp on a few hundred dollars when it is so little in terms of your whole investment? Step into that one four or five times and "whole" is a whole lot larger.

I told myself I could be realistic, face facts, even conquer them. People had said, in theoretical terms, that the house would cost us twice as much as we had planned to spend. Very well, I could adjust: I would simply plan (to myself, of course) to spend double from the very beginning. The trouble with this sort of thinking, obviously, is that there's no place to get off. I was making just about as much sense as the Hollywood star who, when she was told that the picture was three days behind schedule, asked why they hadn't started three days earlier. It is the kind of "shaggy dog" logic that can be very funny—if the consequences aren't serious.

I had honestly tried to face facts, but sometimes I had trouble finding them. I would be told that this would cost less than that: vinyl asbestos tile less than cushioned vinyl, painted wood less than polished wood paneling. My next question, naturally, would be how much less? And that was where it would end. I could never find out how much less. I never knew whether we were talking in terms of hundreds of dollars or thousands. Often estimates require the work of more than one man, and if the project is finally dropped, it all becomes wasted effort. I had to settle for terms like "substantial" increase or decrease and "inconsequential" or "unimportant" difference in price. But this vagueness does leave you with a very uneasy feeling. And I'm sure it encouraged me to feel that we were economizing much more meaningfully than, in fact, we were.

I knew that the price of building a house is reckoned in terms of cost per square foot. So when in the very beginning John and Mike discussed figures, I multiplied and came up with what I thought was an honest total estimate. It was honest as far as it went. What I had neglected to find out was exactly what it covered. And what it didn't. Obviously, it would not include the original cost of the land. I knew that the landscaping and the architect's fee would be extra. However, it was not till much later that I found out that it did not cover the greenhouse, the terrace, the swimming pool or anything else beyond the inside walls. There is, we discovered, no set rule, no professional definition that governs cost per foot. What it pays for varies wildly from contractor to contractor, job to job. It may or may not include hardware, flooring, bookshelves, paneling, kitchen equipment, plumbing and lighting fixtures. Even more confusing, it may include a "normal" or "usual" or "reasonable" amount (whatever that means) of any or all of these. So I pass on our first painfully gained bit of wisdom: before you make final commitments, find out *exactly* what cost per foot means in your case.

My second rule would be: beware of the engineering costs—what goes on between the walls, whether it's plumbing or heating or air-conditioning, electrical or electronic. Don't be put off by the fact that you yourself are not equipped to suggest technical changes. Do make sure that the system you are getting is not sophisticated beyond your real needs. In this department, utter refinement is fabulously expensive.

What else can you do? What did we do?

Well, we sat down and went over the plans again very, very carefully, questioning and eliminating wherever it was possible. Our first decision was to eliminate the paneling in the entrance hall. And once we had done it, I realized the change simplified things for me. Without the limitations imposed by paneling, the wall would be much easier to place furniture against.

We decided to paint all the living-room paneling white. It would save a great deal of money, and, at this stage, that was enough to win me over. Should we decide that we needed color later, it would be a simple matter to repaint.

We took out the radiant heating that was to have been provided for the bathroom floors, and we simplified the air-conditioning zoning. And we substituted the old Rockmeadow generator, which was just enough to keep the greenhouse going, for the new auxiliary system that would have provided minimal power to every part of the house. The flowers were irreplaceable; but even if we were to lose everything in the freezer several times because of power failures, we'd still be financially ahead of what the new generator would have cost.

All this did *not* bring the price of the house within reason. And that brings me to a most important point: building anything today is very, very costly, no matter what the scale. Whether you start out to do a $15,000 remodeling job or to build a whole house, it will cost more, probably much more, than you think. As they are in everything, prices for construction are on the rise, and it looks very much as though they will keep on going up. To keep skilled men, you must pay them very well. There is almost always someone up the road who is willing to pay outrageous "travel" expenses to tempt them off your job and onto his. And you are stuck with it. You may quite legally try to hold a carpenter to the signed estimate on his contract. And if he quits the job because, he says, he is losing money on it, you can take him to court. But both of you will have lost, and you won't have your house.

It is not a pretty picture, but there it is.

Only one fact is more important when you speak of the high cost of building. And that is that spending a great deal of money does not guarantee a beautiful result any more than having limited funds means you must end with something unimaginative and dull. Without work and thinking and caring, no amount of money can buy you a success.

Frankly, if we had known the real picture before we started, money might very possibly have stopped us from building the house. Nothing else could have. Delays can be waited through if you care as much as we did.

However, we were committed, and we went ahead. We have known people who put fantastic sums into raising racehorses or prize cattle. We don't do either, and we don't keep a yacht. Our extravagance has always been money spent on our homes, a tradition which we seem destined to continue. The sum involved was tremendous, but we were extremely fortunate that we had it. And the house was that important to us.

It was more than a house, more than just a shelter. So although we could have economized more—put in wood floors, asphalt roof shingles, standardized door frames—we stopped short of things that would really compromise what it was meant to be.

A house is a house—but this was a dream.

And a dream coming true is priceless.

CHAPTER SIX

Suitcases in the Potting Shed

SPRING came, the weather got warmer, and the house began to look very much like a place you might move into one day. The outer walls were up; the roofs were shingled with slate, and by the first of May, Paul had flowers blooming in the greenhouse. With the front courtyard brought up almost to grade level, the house seemed to have settled comfortably onto the land. The beauty and dignity of its proportions, of roof to walls to broad chimney, were real, not just lines on a drawing. The windows were in and for the first time I could actually (not just in my mind's eye) see through the glass on either side of the front door, across the living room and over the pool to the tops of the trees beyond.

Arriving on those first mild days, I'd pause to enjoy a new set of sensations. I felt welcomed by the entrance, beckoned by the view and sheltered by the two wings formed by the garage wall on one side and the bedroom wing on the other.

Inside, the walls were going up and the living-room ceiling, plastered at last, gave the room which was the focal point of the house three-dimensional reality. Filled with light and air, it had a little the feeling that a floating pavilion must have. The swimming pool, painted white now, made the whole terrace area look nearly finished. Water in the pool from the spring rains heightened the illusions, but meant a new discipline for Roger, the retriever, who would now have to be taught that it was off limits for him.

Rooms Take Shape

There was no denying that it was a big house, although in square footage Rockmeadow was considerably larger. In the winter, when bare trees left an open view from the road, friends would drive by and see its several roofs, then call to ask how work on "the village" was progressing. But as the house took form, the brilliance of John's design proved itself once more. In spite of its over-all size, things were so arranged that you saw only a small part of the house at any one time, and each aspect provided its own delightful surprise: a near view with a cluster of trees framed by a window or a far vista sweeping out to the sky. The views from Dick's room were spectacular: on one side, he would see the pool and, eventually, the garden; on the other, treetops and distant ridges.

With scarcely disguised impatience, I waited to be told when we could move in. Finally, on June 24th, Mike told us that the service wing would be finished on July 8th, and that Dick and I could move into the two maids' rooms the following week. It would certainly not be like having a finished house to live in, but I was ecstatic at the news. The kitchen and pantry would be complete and functioning. Our temporary quarters would be small, but bright and pretty; we'd have the terrace, the screened porches and the swimming pool —and best of all, I would have time to experiment and to get to know all the wonders of my new kitchen.

I promptly worked out a timetable and set the wheels in motion for Stage I of the Big Move. The couple who were to help us had been on call since June 1st, Mike's original deadline for completing the caretaker's room. They would have to be alerted and arrangements made to put them up in the neighborhood so that they could be on hand to unpack as things were delivered. The local warehouse already had a list of cartons and boxes containing things we would need for the service wing; all they needed to know was the final delivery date. I notified the upholsterer and the cabinetmaker and the carpet company so that the cotton rugs as well as the repainted and re-covered furniture could be sent over that second week in July. And, of course, I set to work on dozens of lists, all headed "Don't forget. . . ." There were paper things (towels, cups, plates, napkins), staples (flour, sugar, spices, rice), cleaning supplies (cleansers, soaps, detergents, liquids), and those were only the beginnings. Things were happening at last.

On June 29th, I put down my pencil and pads long enough to go through the morning's mail—and thunder struck. In my hand was a copy of a letter from Mike to John which stated—rather casually, I thought—that the caretaker could move in on July 15th, that Dick and I could have the maids' rooms on the 23rd of July, and that the house would be finished *on October 1st, if the mechanical work was completed by then.*

The shock was total; I had seen no warning lightning. I stared, I reread, I despaired—then I settled things in a very feminine fashion by bursting into tears. I had been promised that if I worked, and the weather held. . . . Well, I had worked, and we had had the warmest winter in memory. We knew (and had been reminded) that some delays were inevitable, and we had been, I thought, rather good-humored about them so far. But I, for one, had just about run out of humor. I wanted our house.

I was prepared to be reasonable—I know because it says so in my notes: "I am even willing to concede that if the guest rooms aren't ready for occupancy until the very end, it will be relatively minor. As long as Dick's room and mine and the baths and dressing rooms and the living room are ready, we will be able to get a great deal of pleasure out of the house, even if we can't put up overnight guests."

Looking back at those notes, I smile, but I don't mean it. Even from this distance, it isn't funny; but in view of what came later, there is a certain comedy in my naïve faith that what I was facing up to was Reality.

"Surely, this is some terrible kind of joke," I wailed to John on the phone. "Mike just can't mean it. He said a house for the summer, and that isn't . . . can't be . . . he *couldn't* mean October first."

On the other end of the wire, John sounded calm, but was, I suspect, almost as concerned as I. He called Mike, then called me back with reassurance. It wasn't as bad as it looked on paper, he said; he felt that Mike was trying to cover himself. The couple could still move in, if not on the 8th, on the day after; and Dick and I could be in the following week. On the surface, everything seemed smoothed out—surely, one day's delay was not very important. Still, after all John's soothing talk, one large blank remained to be filled in: the date on which the entire house would really be finished.

I said all I could, put all the pressure I could on John and Mike. Then I had to be content with talking, whispering, shouting to myself. I wouldn't go sobbing to Dick. It wasn't simply a matter of his being busy. It was also that I knew that this sort of thing was just what he'd had in mind when he had offered so long ago to go away for a year if I was going to build a house. It was all that emotional wear and tear. So my own pride and promises kept me somewhat silent while I tried everything I could think of to move things along.

First, I tried modified patience. With John, who hadn't been up in some time, I visited the house, and we went over every unfinished detail with Mike. At the end of our consultation, I felt better although I had still not been given a firm completion date. Somehow it seemed that everything was back on the track. Having done all I could to prepare for the move, I would be quiet and wait.

The 8th came and went, and the 9th. John and Margit, the couple who were to look after the house for us, still had no room to call home. But Pearl, who had been with us at Rockmeadow and was standing by to help at the new house, had kindly taken them into her home. The things from the warehouse arrived minus only a few of the cartons we needed and with only a few unasked-for items added. All this was stashed in the maids' rooms and in the potting shed along with some furniture from New York. Nothing could be put in place, of course; but it was there. And teams of men working —laying floors, painting walls, placing cabinets and ceiling skylights —gave rise to faint hopes that progress was being made.

Emotionally, it was possibly the most mercurial time in all my life. My mood swung from despair to delight and back depending on the day's news from or visit to Connecticut. On Wednesday, July 13th, to take just one small example, my diary reads simply: "Chaos, delay, disappointment, errors . . . Very upset . . . Home, very depressed." My day's trip to the country had, obviously, revealed any number of mistakes and omissions, some of them in the kitchen, but an overwhelming majority in the laundry.

I might just as well not have bothered with laundry plans. The logical order John and I had discussed was nowhere to be found. I never actually saw a final plan, but my open shelves (the ones for stacking fresh linen) had vanished into a solid wall of cabinets. The shelves to hold nice big laundry baskets had turned into several built-in cabinet-type hampers, immobile and far too small. Some hanging space had disappeared entirely, and the deep and admittedly old-fashioned laundry tubs of my dreams had become sleek stainless-steel sinks which provided ample depth for soaking a pair of matched handkerchiefs. The catalogue of errors went on, and on. "Depressed" was scarcely the word for the way I felt.

Yet two days later, on Friday the 15th, the same woman, in the same diary, reports, "I went to the country with John, and we worked on the problems of the laundry and kitchen. I had been so upset about minor things (a great many of them) and the delay. . . . But I have a feeling we accomplished a great deal. I feel much happier about everything." Thus my schizophrenia progressed.

Meanwhile I was waging psychological war. My intuition told me that unless we made a tremendous effort to establish residence, the delaying tactics would continue indefinitely. So, since we had set July 15th as the day to move in, I clung to it right down the line. On the 13th (Chaos Day), still trying to believe we would need them in forty-eight hours, I brought out two suitcases full of Dick's and my clothes. There was obviously no place to unpack them since both of the bedrooms we had planned to use were piled ceiling high with crates and cartons of things that would be moved out "as soon as" the walls and the floors and the ceilings in the kitchen were finished and the cabinets and equipment installed. But I was determined that I would not take so much as one overnight bag back to New York. So into the potting shed went the luggage to wait for our arrival.

Just knowing those cases were there helped ease the day's discouragements a little. In the back of my mind was the thought that when Mike saw them, he'd know I was serious. And every time he passed them, they would act as reminders.

We did not move in on Friday, July 15th. I could have stamped my feet and shouted and got people to scurry about, but it wouldn't have done any good. The rooms were finally cleared, and there were beds and some of the furniture in them. However, the air-conditioning was not hooked up; the hot-water system had just been tested;

and, on the whole, John seemed so concerned about mechanics in general that we conceded and put off the Move for a week. With the suitcases in the potting shed establishing a beachhead, I felt that we could afford to be a bit generous.

On Sunday the 17th, we did have a beautiful picnic. Mary's husband, Hank, who had never been able to visit the house before, came along. And all that bright summer afternoon we basked on the terrace and swam. The swimming was blissful. There were the wings of the house for shelter, yet as you floated in the pool you were hypnotized by the wide sky above and the distant view beyond. That day, for the first time, Dick seemed excited. I suspect that up to that point he hadn't actually been able to convince himself that we would ever move in. Now, I think, he really believed it would happen. For both of us, it made all the difference. And before we left for New York, I went to work in the maids' rooms that were to be ours for a while. I plugged in the lamps, wound the clocks, rescued the suitcases from the shed and unpacked.

Our First Night in the House

The 21st—a shiny, clear Thursday—was the day that shall live in glory. I drove up early that morning and, armed with a list that was almost as long as the road from the house to Fairfield, I set out for Mercurio's Market to lay in staples and supplies. I love just about everything that has to do with food and cooking, but I've never enjoyed any shopping trip as much as I did that one. The thought of flour and rice in the cupboards, butter in the refrigerator and ice cream in the freezer was almost too exciting to bear. Pearl and I stacked the shelves all the rest of the afternoon. And then, about five, Dick finally arrived.

I wish I could honestly say that he found me fresh and enchanting, waiting to welcome him with a cool drink and a little something supperish (sorrel soup and a filet would have been nice). He found me elated but exhausted—willing and just about able to be taken out for dinner. But the glorious fact remained: that night we spent our very first night in The House.

The next morning I woke at five, partly because I was too excited to sleep, and partly because, I suppose, some interior alarm clock told me that the workmen would be arriving at eight and I didn't want to be hurried through our first breakfast. Everything worked—including the number of footsteps (a very few) from burners to sink to dishwasher to counter. The longest trip of the morning was across the kitchen to the refrigerator—a matter of some twelve feet. The cushioned vinyl floor covering was not only wonderfully comfortable and quiet underfoot, but I discovered it also kept dropped dishes from breaking. (Its only drawback seemed to be that it didn't show dirt.) I was bathed, dressed and had breakfast served and cleared away long before the first of the workmen's cars turned into the driveway outside.

Everything went beautifully for us that weekend. The rooms were airy and comfortable; the beds, marvelous. And although the air-conditioning still wasn't prepared to function, the weather was so clear and cool it didn't matter. We shopped and worked and swam. The pool was so accessible and inviting that Dick, who hadn't been in Rockmeadow's pool for years, actually got up at seven to take his first dip on Saturday. As he explained to friends who dropped by later, "It's like having a kind of luxurious playhouse." And it was—almost incredibly so. That first Sunday morning when Dick was sitting by the pool with his breakfast tray, the scene was so much the way we had planned it that I could hardly believe my eyes.

As for my recreation, between emptying cartons and washing kitchen equipment, I managed to cook up a storm. It was like owning a toy store, all new—I just couldn't wait to see how everything worked. I baked to test the ovens (though I was a little timid about trying the self-cleaning part). Next day I did a chicken with sauce supreme and rice. I left the sauce in the double boiler, put the chicken and rice in the warming drawer, and when we came in from swimming, it was just as deliciously warm as the ads had promised. The meat was moist, the rice was fluffy with every grain standing on its own. I couldn't wait to try the drawers with a roast of beef.

As weekends went by, I got around to auditioning all the kitchen's new marvels. I must admit there were moments when I felt that a degree from M.I.T. would have been a big help. The first time I tried the self-cleaning oven, it didn't; but my second try produced sensational results. (As time passed, we discovered serious cooking problems, and though the manufacturers were as eager as we to solve them, it took a long time.) Then there was the time the pilot light on the charcoal broiler went out (the instruction manual was *not* in the drawer after all) and left me holding the lamb chops. Once the dishwasher refused to function because I had overstuffed its detergent cup, and a whole cake of soap did manage to slip into the garbage disposer when I wasn't looking (cleverly, I did not reach in after it). But generally, things worked beautifully, and I would go off to bed at night with the dishwasher washing, the oven cleaning and the jets vacuuming the pool. It gave me the feeling that an army of very small robots was working while I slept. (In all honesty I should point out that when we received the estimates for what the brochure described as a "self-vacuuming pool," a vacuum was included and I was told that "of course, the pool will have to be vacuumed at least once every two weeks." And, after the installation had been completed, we learned to our great disappointment that although the pool did not need to be vacuumed as frequently as the "old-fashioned" filtered pool, at the time this book went to press almost daily brushing was required to keep the pool as sparkling as the pictures in the advertising brochure.)

Without doubt, the "toy" I had most fun with was the freezer. There was a certain joy in just standing and looking at its well-fed interior. To a base of favorite commercially prepared foods like those delicious young vegetables that come in plastic bags ready to pop into boiling water, I had added extra supplies of meat and butter, muffins and bread and rolls. There were lobster and brook trout, frozen chives and parsley and dill. And of course I had stocked up on ice cream and sherbet. But by far the most satisfying section contained a growing collection of home-produced items that ranged from sauce to an ice-cream-filled chocolate roll and frozen pastry shells ready for the oven. There was court-bouillon saved from the bass I had done and all sorts of soup stock frozen in ice trays, then the cubes emptied into plastic bags. In fact, I became the first person I've ever heard of to be wounded by that universal healer, chicken soup. It happened when a bag of frozen cubes of same slipped out of my hand and fell to the floor, bruising my shin on the way.

Everything in the freezer was wrapped in usable portions and labeled. I had planned to buy a blackboard on which to keep a list of contents, but John suggested a handier way of keeping track. So I now use a grease pencil called a "China Marker" (it's the kind hardware stores use to put prices on pots and pans), and I write on the inside of the enameled door of the cupboard next to the freezer. As things are used, I correct the list with the wipe of a damp cloth: nothing could be easier. The contents of the freezer grew and prospered, and almost without knowing it, I was launched on a whole new system of cooking and entertaining.

Meanwhile, Monday morning came. We stayed long enough to go over a list of needed adjustments with Mike, then started for the city. My feet and back ached, and I was feeling muscles I hadn't used for years. I was really ready for a few days of city rest. Yet, bone tired as I was, when it came time to leave I resented having to go. It had been a glorious weekend—one of the happiest of our lives.

Still, there were plenty of New York errands that needed to be taken care of. Some, like calling stores about furniture that had been delivered damaged, were simply chores. But there were pleasant jobs too. These had to do with our new walls and things to hang on them. In the winter I had browsed through gallery after gallery and found several things we both liked, including a small three-dimensional op-art work by Freund that is great fun to look at plus two moody paintings by an artist new to me, Robert Kipness. The screened dining and sitting areas presented special problems. There were three big walls to consider—each of them twelve feet long. Obviously, since they would be exposed to rain, wind and cold, paintings were out. For one I found a beautiful long narrow serigraph by Victor Passmore. Then I set off to search for other things, in ceramic, or bronze, or I-wasn't-quite-sure-what. At the Museum of Contemporary Crafts, I saw hundreds of transparencies of works by American artists, and I was especially drawn to the work of Glen Michaels, a Michigan man who has done some striking ceramic wall sculptures. Through the Museum, I was able to get in touch with him and arrange for him to visit the house on his next trip to New York.

Meanwhile, on weekends, free from the sort of schedule that having servants imposes on any household, we had the house to ourselves—a real luxury and a delight, though sometimes a hectic and exhausting one. I baked and brewed and poached, burned my fingers, wore my feet out and had a lovely time.

Our principal reason for moving into the service wing before the rest of the house was finished was so that we could enjoy at least part of the summer. But aside from the pleasure it gave us, our decision turned out to be a wise one in several practical ways. I was able to get to know all the equipment before having to show someone else how to use it. Also, I feel very strongly that if you are building a house, or a room, or re-designing your kitchen, you should be there as much as possible while the work is in progress. Neither the architect nor the contractor can give the kind of time-consuming supervision that is essential. To be sure, the architect's detailed drawings and the contractor's ability to transfer those drawings to the actual house, room or cabinet are of primary importance. But if you care deeply about the finished work, make yourself available to answer the questions that always arise in spite of careful planning.

The Importance of Being on Hand

To give an example of the kind of thing I mean: on the blueprint for one bathroom, the toilet-paper holder was located quite properly in the wall to the right of the toilet. However, when the workmen tried to install it, they found it wouldn't fit in the precise spot indicated because of a duct buried in the wall. So they decided to put the holder in the wall opposite the toilet almost out of reach. Fortunately, I was there, and found that with a little juggling it could be set into the wall where it belonged after all.

When I discovered small mistakes, I could have them corrected on the spot. As anyone who has ever tried it knows, it is virtually impossible to get any workman to return to a job once he has left it. But in our case, masons, plumbers, electricians and painters were on hand every Monday morning and able to deal with any "bugs" that might have come to light in the course of the weekend. Also, I hoped that our presence might stimulate everyone to work a little harder to finish things up. And if that dream could come true, it was worth any small discomfort we might have to put up with.

There was one final advantage: when it came time to have the rest of our furniture delivered, the back-breaking part of the unpacking job—getting the china, the glasses and the silver washed and put away, opening and laundering linens—would be done. Clothes we were not using for the time being hung in the two big closets in the entrance hall, ready to be transferred to the dressing rooms. After that, all that was left to do was place the furniture, put away books and hang the pictures. When the moment came, we should, I thought, be in good shape very quickly.

This is not to say that joy reigned unconfined. It most certainly did not. Witness, for example, this hot July blast:

"There was a point," say my notes, "when I worried that the book might be too full of sweetness and light and everyone loving everyone, and everything going smoothly. Forget it! is the message of today."

Delaying Tactics and Diversionary Activities

Each weekend we could see progress, yet a finished house remained something far, far away. Faced with rising costs and delays that were always "unavoidable," my feeling of impotence was overwhelming. I talked to myself, lots, in paragraphs that began, "When a contractor tells you that he can build a house in seven months . . ." and "When an architect says you can have a house . . ." and "When a subcontractor gives you a date and then blandly denies he ever set it . . ." I was still sure we would have a wonderful house eventually. But the question was "When?"

This sort of frustration comes to everyone who builds a house, but I had somehow managed to convince myself that we wouldn't have to face it. The infuriating fact is that no amount of farsightedness on your part helps. It is impossible for you to control the work as it is actually being done.

There had been some shipping delays. The doors from Spain had lost some necessary papers en route which slowed their arrival a bit. The French roller blinds got as far as the customs shed in New York before they were stopped because the bill of lading called for ten crates and only nine had walked off the plane. It was, it seemed, against all rules to open the nine crates before the tenth was found—even when it was pointed out that since nothing was labeled, we wouldn't know what was missing until we did investigate. In any case, it would have taken months to replace the missing parts. After a series of cables to and from France, the manufacturer suggested we go straight to the airline and imply, emphatically, that we would file a substantial claim for loss and inconvenience. Miraculously, the missing crate came to the surface in Brooklyn, and that problem was solved.

Our beautiful black Japanese stones made it out of the river, across the sea and as far as New York before the burlap bags containing our order got integrated with someone else's shipment of small white pebbles. But since the mistake had been made so close to home, it was relatively easy to locate the remainder of our order.

After considerable exotic correspondence (one letter addressed to Mrs. Richard Rodgers began, "Dear Sir" and ended, "Hoping be received this rugs in perfectly condicitions, I am . . .") our Spanish rugs arrived pretty much on schedule. But nothing could be that simple. I learned from my carpet man here in New York that each one would have to be cleaned before it was laid; otherwise the animal oils remaining in the wool would give us streaking problems ever after.

The fact is that all these hold-ups were relatively minor; nothing I had ordered slowed progress on the house. The delays I found so incomprehensible were those that came about through lack of supervision or attention to plans; or through failure to look ahead and realize when certain things would be needed and should be ordered, or when things that had been ordered had not arrived.

Time and again my irritation focused on the kitchen and the laundry. To take just one recurrent instance, I have no idea how often or how many people I reminded that in the kitchen, the pantry and the galley of the caretaker's quarters, space should be set aside for can openers, drying racks for linen towels, dispensers for waxed paper, foil and paper towels. Yet nothing was done until so late that none could be properly placed. It was inconceivable to me that in these days of refined functional systems, the problem of finding a good container for such necessities—things you use a dozen times in fixing any meal—should be considered so unimportant that they could be ignored. With the cabinets set and the ducts (for air-conditioning, etc.) buried in the walls, there was literally no place left to set in such small but essential pieces of equipment.

It seems to me that designers have got sidetracked on over-refinements. They have, for example, moved range controls so that they are out of children's reach but so placed that in turning them on adult arms come dangerously close to the burners. It would be much more sensible to teach children not to touch stoves. Common everyday needs are forgotten. Experts don't plan kitchen drawers to hold both long and short-handled utensils; they have yet to provide an alternative to stacking cups in their sleek new metal cabinets, and they've devised no really convenient system for storing bottles of herbs and spices if you don't, as I don't, care to keep them in racks along the wall.

But my deepest frustration lay in the fact that no matter how often I reminded or pleaded, no one from the kitchen-planning firm seemed concerned about correcting existing mistakes. Dents and scratches remained in cupboard doors, unwanted shelves were not removed and the inefficient wine-rack arrangement that had been put in without my approval wasn't changed until I got around to doing it myself. We had given the kitchen designers ninety percent of their estimate as an advance in order to take advantage of a prepayment discount. It was a mistake I will never repeat. Now they seemed completely indifferent.

On the other hand, most of the men on the job took great pride in their work. They had always been neat and careful. But, from the moment we moved in, they seemed to take special care to leave the place swept up and tidy. It was a completely cooperative effort.

Fridays and Mondays were work days, the days I checked progress and plans with Mike and, although it took me some time to realize it, the days on which I received instruction in a whole new language. What fooled me at first was that it sounded so much like English. But in time I came to realize that, in contractor talk, the most familiar-seeming words had entirely new connotations. Phrases I had found reassuring only weeks before became warning signals, ringing bells and bristling with red lights and flags. Unreasonable as it may seem, there was a time when, to me, the phrase "just as soon as" (as in "just as soon as the bookcases come, we'll go right through, laying floors, painting, finishing up") implied completion in the foreseeable future (as of bookcases coming *this week*). Given this unreal premise, my mind raced on to visions of jet-propelled people flying about, accomplishing this and this, till there was our house—all done. Obviously, I was wrong; those words meant no such thing. While "as soon as" did promise a sequence of actions once the bookcases materialized, it implied nothing whatever about the timing of their arrival. It was not even a certain sign that they had been ordered.

Once I learned this lesson, I adopted new tactics—only to come up against a new set of diversionary techniques that would have done *South Pacific's* Luther Billis proud. The first was the positive non-sequitur, or one-good-question-deserves-another response. Having been told that such-and-such a thing would happen "as soon as the bookcases come," I would come back smartly: "When *are* the book-cases coming?" This earned me a no-answer like, "What's happened to the hardware for the front door?" And suddenly we would be off on another tack.

Second, there was the old-fashioned buck pass:

"When," I would ask, "is the air-conditioning going to be hooked up?"

"Well," would come the response, "a man's going to have to test it, and that takes at least three days."

"All right," I'd say quietly, "when are they going to start testing it?"

"Well, the union tells me how many men I can have. And so far they've only allowed me enough to go on with the main job—no extras to start testing. So what are we going to do?" Unfortunately, no one around seemed to have a sign like the one Mr. Truman had, saying, "The Buck Stops Here."

Having been told of Mike's day-to-day log, I realized how many problems he had solved without even letting us know that they existed. There had been inter-union quarrels and several strikes which, because of his adroit timing, had not slowed our progress by even so much as a day. Our roofs, for example, were rushed through and finished the evening before roofers all over the state stopped work for a week. Yet, grateful as I was for these things, what I came to recognize as the Delaying Game continued to plague me—particularly since, no matter how cleverly I tried to compete, I never seemed to win.

I don't remember exactly when it was that I gave up pursuing a "final" completion date. It must have been after the frightful hot spell we had that summer. The weather cooled off, and so did I when I realized how much energy I was expending trying to pry a commitment from a source that clearly would not or could not give me one.

Besides, we were having a lovely time. We were terribly comfortable in our "borrowed" rooms—in fact, several times Dick said he wasn't sure he'd be willing to move when our own bedrooms were ready. The porches, the bedrooms, the kitchen and pantry made a very compact and convenient unit. The furniture in the dining-sitting area of the kitchen proved to be extremely comfortable and practical. There was a dining table with a white Formica top and four black iron legs; vinyl-covered swivel chairs (some black and some white); a pair of armless chairs in buttoned black vinyl with chrome bases; and two handsome red lamps on tables with plastic tops. It had taken a bit of looking, and I had to wait six to eight weeks for delivery, but the design of the furniture was excellent and the prices were reasonable. There was also a television set, and I had my built-in desk and a telephone, so we really had all the comforts of home.

We had no house guests, and we missed having the children out (Linda and Danny and Peter were on the West Coast, and it was a long drive from Mary and Hank's summer place to come just for the day). But our Saturdays and Sundays were pleasant, if slightly hectic. Friends who wanted to see the house came in a steady stream for drinks, lunch and, very occasionally, dinner. Before, after and during their visits a parade of workmen passed through on routine or emergency errands. A sample Saturday's list of arrivals included the DeVrieses, the Knopfs, the Darrows, the Herseys, the Pabsts and the Heyns, plus the TV man, the gas man, the pool people and a policeman who wanted Dick to autograph a record album. The traffic was nothing if not brisk and varied, and Dick and I ran guided tours on the half-hour.

To my relief and delight, although the house was far from finished, almost everyone who came to see it seemed to get its message; they managed not only to say the right things, but to sound very much as though they meant them. We had very few "That *is* a baby" comments. There were exceptions, of course (one long-time friend seemed quite miffed that the house wasn't the "cottage" she felt we had led her to expect). But there were many more people who found it "airy" and "peaceful" and "beautiful, modern but still so warm"; and women, especially, understood and admired the ease with which it would (someday) work. Each group left us tired but glowing.

The End Is in Sight

Week by week, things were accomplished. The terrace was finished and Miss Smith did more planting. The bookcases *did* come, the floor tiles *were* laid (and I must say they looked glorious), the painters *did* arrive. Our seventh weekend in the house would be Labor Day, and I was told that the Thursday before, the living room and the entrance hall would be finished, all ready for furniture.

Having advised the warehouse people in New York and in Connecticut, I could hardly wait for the morning to arrive. We drove up from the city late Wednesday night to be there first thing in the morning when the vans were due. I took a flashlight and went in to admire the completed living room only to discover that all the cabinetwork *wasn't* finished, there were still doors to be hung and some of the painting hadn't even been started. Thursday morning the New York van, carrying all the things I'd acquired in the past few months, pulled in, as promised, on the dot of ten; by one, all its beautifully organized contents were unloaded and set in place. The two local vans, loaded with things from Rockmeadow, were quite a different story. They were due to arrive at one-thirty. It was five o'clock, however, before they finally lumbered up the driveway, and by that time, having been forced to sit, doing nothing, for three and a half hours, I would not have been in the best of moods had everything been in perfect condition. What I found was complete disorder. There were lists of what was being delivered, but they were impossible to check and there was no one in the group to direct the unloading. Things I had asked for didn't appear, and several pieces that did, things quite precious to us, had been badly packed and, as a consequence, cracked or broken in transit. I found myself unpacking a case of family photographs and papers—but not our family's. Starting so late, it was a back-breaking task to get bedroom things stored in the shed and the living-room things in place. We were all running so fast that there was no time to stand back and survey, to see if things were turning out at all as I had pictured them.

Friday morning the living room was alive with painters, electricians, carpenters, plumbers, three women hanging curtains, and me. While they fitted, dabbed and hammered away on the finishing touches, I unpacked books into the cases, not in any sort of scholarly order, but so that we would have color instead of blank shelves to look at. I had taken all the lamps that needed new shades (it's curious, but lampshade styles do change) to the local lamp shop in a couple of station-wagon loads (a feat that would have been impossible in the city). Now they were back and ready to be put in place.

At four o'clock, the witching hour on any construction job, everyone faded away to start his holiday weekend and left me with only a few more cartons to deal with. These held all the ornaments from Rockmeadow—the china and small pictures, the needlepoint pillows and bits of sculpture, things we had collected, lived with and loved for years. I placed them around the room—the Judy Brown musicians on the new bar-buffet, the framed Coptic embroidery on the fruitwood piece across from it, a Dali drawing on the table behind the long sofa. I spread the small pillows around, set out cigarettes, ashtrays and matches. Then Paul brought in pots of plants, including some beautiful geraniums for the long Venetian red table, and the living room was done.

I was almost afraid to look. Suppose, in spite of my planning, things looked awful. The colors, the scale, the groupings might be wrong. And because I was so anxious to have Dick like it, I was terrified for fear he wouldn't.

When I did look, I was happy with what I saw; Dick loved it. As though he wanted to go on "discovering," he would move from one part of the room to another; sit in this chair, then that one, as if to enjoy it from all angles. It wouldn't have been real without one mistake, and I had made that in the beautiful rug I had ordered as a skirt for a small table. Somehow the rug was the wrong shape, and no amount of re-working would have made it right. So I was doubly fortunate: first, that I had another table I could substitute for the one I had originally planned to use; and second, that the rug was so beautiful and salable that there was no problem about returning it.

Otherwise, all was serene—especially Jacqueline Picasso, who looked beautiful over the fireplace (John Stonehill said that he was sure people would think I had added her green hair ribbon myself just to tone in with the color scheme). We had brought two other paintings from New York to try in the room. There was a Graham Sutherland with a background that was almost the same color as the geraniums in the table and in the tubs around the pool. It had hung for years in the dining room of the apartment, where it was almost wasted. Now, hung in the thrust part of the room, where it is the first thing you see as you come in from the hall, it is a spectacular success. The second painting, a gentle, romantic Zao-Wou-Ki, hung across from it, where it contributes a subtle kind of tranquillity.

Though Dick's reaction was the one that really mattered, I was delighted when friends, seeing the room for the first time, called it "cozy" in spite of its size. It was exactly the feeling I had hoped it would have. What surprised me was that friends who had seen it unfurnished confessed that they never dreamed that such a large room could possibly be made warm and livable. (Evidently the word-pictures I had painted on guided tours had not been as clear for others as they were to me.) Much of the warmth was due to the contents of those last cartons—the bits and pieces of what Dick calls "cheerful clutter" from Rockmeadow. I'm sure they were responsible for several people's remarking that the room didn't have "that new look. . . . It's as though these things had always been here."—which, to me, meant they looked at home. One comment I'll treasure forever came from Jennifer Crichton, my niece Judy's nine-year-old daughter, who compared ours to the only other new house she had ever seen, a rather elaborate neo-Tudor mansion. "I like yours much better," said Jenny. "Theirs is a copy, but yours is an original. Besides, theirs is too *good* for you. . . . I mean there's really no place where you dare to sit down."

Reactions like that made it worth all the nuisance of storing everything fragile away in cupboards every Sunday night and setting it all out again the next Friday afternoon. But all those weeks while there were still workmen in the house—painting, fitting doors and putting in the alarm system—and breakage was a distinct possibility, things had to be done that way.

Mechanical Problems

While visually all was calm, mechanically things were anything but. One Friday morning just after seven, a sudden deafening silence descended. Actually, I found it rather pleasant until it dawned on me that it really meant that something was very wrong. Sure enough, when we investigated, we found there wasn't a watt of power anywhere in the house. Mike was as puzzled as we were until we discovered that the failure was town-wide and not the fault of a quirk in our own wiring. At nine-thirty the lights came on again and everyone stopped worrying.

We shouldn't have, for, it developed, this was only the beginning of a series of incidents that have transformed the phrase "at the flick of a switch" (words that, to my ears, once connoted ease and comfort) to a warning, a baleful omen of mechanical crises to come. My conditioning was gradual. At five-thirty that same afternoon, Pearl appeared to report there was no hot water. It was not until Saturday night that Mike and one of the plumbers succeeded in turning on the boiler. Someone had accidentally turned it off with the flick of a switch. So, surrounded by miles of sophisticated systems, I had to take my baths in water heated in a teakettle on the stove.

Frank Carroll, who was in charge of installing the plumbing, heating and air-conditioning, was careful to explain to us that we must be patient—a word for which, about this time, I had developed a full-blown loathing. Both John and Mike had already told us that as long as only part of the power-and-heating complex was being used, the system would be impossible to control. We could not expect perfection until the whole mechanical system (by which they meant all those pipes and ducts I would never understand) was complete and functioning throughout the house. Then, we were assured, all would be well. And this would be an accomplished fact in less than two weeks' time (it was now early October).

Some of our troubles were laid on the mammoth shoulders of an enormous power-devouring monster that lived in the basement and was referred to, in true science-fiction fashion, as "EC - 5"; it seemed he was responsible for all sorts of foibles, including occasional dim-outs. He was clearly to blame for all the problems having to do with air-conditioning and its zoning. Sometimes he went off into a beautiful quiet sulk; the only trouble with that was that at those times the air-conditioning went off too. Although I've never seen it happen, I'm sure that when I'm not looking he still lumbers around the cellar like some kind of robot with an angry red eye lit up.

Otherwise, so many of our mechanical malfunctions were attributed to "Somebody" who had "thrown the wrong switch" that I became convinced the cellar was further inhabited by a whole colony of pygmy switch-hitters who worked overtime on Fridays to provide us with weekend surprises. There was, for instance, the Indian-summer weekend on which we arrived to find the house producing its own ninety-degree heat. Thanks to open windows and fans, we managed to temper its fever to eighty by the next morning. But it was not restored to anything like normal until a full day later. It developed, of course, that Somebody had been at it again and had managed to throw the switch that substituted heat for air-cooling. Naturally, a month or so later when the frost was all over Connecticut pumpkins, Somebody arranged an encore and flicked the switch again—this time giving us air-conditioning instead of warmth and threatening us with instant pneumonia. Meanwhile one morning, just to keep us on our toes, the garbage disposer unit became indisposed, the new coffee maker stopped perking and I smashed a pot of nice gooey strawberry jam all over the kitchen table, a chair, the floor, the wall and a curtain. (If it hadn't been for their new miracle surfaces, all these would have been ruined or at least devilish to clean. As it was, I wiped them spotless in minutes, providing the one cheery moment of the day.)

The most crushing blow fell the day all the power in the house had been turned off for fifteen minutes so that the men could do some work on the lightning rods. When everything was switched on again, Somebody failed to push one circuit breaker far enough to make proper contact. Days too late to save anything, we learned that the entire contents of the freezer were spoiled and would have to be thrown out—a total loss not only of money, but of all those hours and my beautiful fish stock, an ice-cream bombe I had so patiently filled with grated chocolate, the pastry shells, a filet of beef and ever so much more.

Delights, Planned and Unexpected

All this was trying, to put it *very* mildly, but the bonuses and pleasures outweighed the trials. We discovered totally unexpected delights—and we're still finding them. The roller blinds were a smashing success. There were small joys—like the movement of the water in the pool (caused by the jet cleaners); so close to the house it provides in summer the same sort of hypnotic perpetual change that you find in a winter fire. The acoustics in the living room are superb, and Dick found a lovely suntrap on the terrace by the dining porch, so protected from the wind that it should stay beautifully warm all winter.

The quality of light throughout the house is quite extraordinary. The screened daylight that falls through a skylight is so different from that which slants in through windows. Spring, summer, fall and winter, there's a fascinating, almost continual change of intensity that moves, in a row of skylights, from the first, to the next, then the next as the earth turns away from the sun. And from outside, there is the unexpected beauty of the bubble-tops at night throwing light up to silhouette the roofs and chimneys (I wonder how they look from the air).

I have become much more emotionally involved with this house than I ever was with Rockmeadow, which, like every other house we had ever lived in, was adopted. This house we had helped to create and we had watched grow. Even though we fumed when progress slowed down, we loved it not only because it was our own but because it fitted us so well.

And work did proceed in spite of one personally crippling setback. The Monday after the first weekend in October, it was raining, and the driveway was wet and slicked here and there by patches of fallen leaves. Cheered by the news that we would have our own bedrooms to sleep in the following weekend, Dick and I were in the car ready to leave for the city when I remembered that I hadn't given the painter approval on a final shade of blue for my room. I know better than to run on slippery pavement, but that didn't stop me. And when I hit a spot of leaves, down I went with knees bent at an angle no self-respecting knees should ever assume. I limped to the bedroom, okayed a color that might well have been red for all I knew—my right leg was hurting so by that time—and managed to make it back to the car. I had, we later found, torn a tendon which pulled a piece of bone loose.

The subsequent weeks in the hospital and the crutches that followed were infuriatingly confining. But if such an accident had to happen, I was lucky that it had waited till that weekend. For, as it turned out, the decision on the paint was literally the last I had to make about the house. So, when the rooms were ready, the rugs were put down; and, with the help of lists and the graph-paper diagrams, Pearl had the furniture set in place.

I don't know what I would have done without Pearl. All the time I was trapped in the city, she was my eyes and ears. Only through her was I able to keep in touch with day-to-day progress (or lack of it) in the country. When, almost six weeks later, I was at last able to return to the house, she was my legs and extra hands as we hung the paintings and placed the rest of the ornaments.

Once again I found I was extremely lucky. Even the two-step changes in level I had pictured when we first started making plans would have made my getting around in a wheelchair impossibly awkward. But with no steps at all to cope with, I found I could really move about very well, though it was maddening not to be able to zip from here to there to adjust a picture or move even the lightest chair without calling for help.

The bedroom wing worked out wonderfully. I had really worried about the Hong Kong carpet I had ordered for the hallway. Its vivid red-and-black pattern could have been a disaster. As John said, it would have been much easier to choose something safe. But we got away with it. Seen from the entrance hall (we haven't hung a door on the bedroom side and John *still* considers this an "error"), the color and design are inviting rather than overpowering. The effect of the carpet combined with the hall's generous width makes you feel it is a place to pause and look at things—the painted Swiss piece that held the hi-fi at Rockmeadow, for instance; the secretary from the living room with pieces of china in it—not just a long space to pass through.

At the end near the guest entrance, there's a telephone with a comfortable chair, a floor lamp and a small table where guests with phoning to do can have peace and privacy. It is also convenient to the croquet field, in case of calls during a game. But we hope the walkie-talkie set, which Dick and I tested in a series of windblown conversations and through which messages can be relayed from players to people inside, will keep phone trips to a minimum.

Dick loved his room—especially the views. And except for the fact that the blue I had chosen that fateful day did turn out to be a bit strong, I was very pleased with mine. In the double guest room, the mauve headboards from Rockmeadow, which I thought might have to be re-covered, looked just right.

Where the bedrooms were concerned, I had only one minor hindsight regret: we had never considered raising the heights of the washbasins which, since this is a house built for grownups, might have made the bathrooms more convenient. Otherwise, things were fine. The overlapping dry-wall construction had given us smooth, relatively soundproof walls that were not only considerably less expensive than plaster but which, I could be happily sure, would never crack. And though there were still men banging away in the basement (the quoted two weeks' completion time had now stretched to six weeks plus), we had our house.

It was a little strange to find myself out of the kitchen and being waited on (Inez and Margaret, our cook and waitress, had come up with us and, pleased though a bit dazed by the newness of things, were making themselves at home). But, being forced to slow down, I could look around me and see it all once more.

I was struck again by how much we owed to John—all the light (incredible through the living-room windows in the morning, through the skylights all day) and the patterns that the house makes (one small example is the little storehouse he placed at the corner of the courtyard to give it definition and extend the lines of the house). There is a pervading tranquillity that comes not only from the unity of materials used throughout the house, but from the serene feeling that grows from having everything on one level; the tile of the living-room floor, the water in the pool and the flagstone of the terrace.

Everywhere the openness of his design invites you to enjoy both the room in which you are sitting and beauty in the spaces beyond. A brilliant Alan Davie watercolor hung in the bedroom hall gives pleasure to people on the screened sitting porch. The Glen Michaels wall sculpture, an intriguing mosaic of slate and shale and ceramic, a perfect complement to the house, has been hung on the porch where, seen through the hall and living-room windows, it is a delight in any weather. For Christmas, Dick and I gave each other an iron sculpture by Somaini which, although abstract, suggests a great bird poised for flight; placed on the corner of the terrace wall, it becomes a thrilling part of the view from the terrace, from Dick's room, my room and even parts of the croquet field. In fact, the house lends itself so beautifully to outdoor sculpture that we hope to add a number of pieces in the next few years.

I felt an enormous sense of pleasure and independence about the house. Though I certainly didn't plan to run it all by myself, the summer had given me confidence that I could really manage it without a great deal of help. In fall, the water in the pool remained blue and clear even after the filter had been turned off; and, thanks to new construction methods, we didn't have to float logs. The pond in the valley was coming into view, and even with the trees bare, things looked beautiful.

Nothing had been said about winter weekends until Dick mentioned buying a Jeep station wagon that could provide us with all-weather transportation. It seemed that neither of us felt we could bear to be separated from the house from late fall till spring. With each week that passes, we seem to belong to it more. Dick says that on Monday mornings he starts planning the return trip before we are out of the driveway. And, as usual, he is speaking for us both.

CHAPTER SEVEN

Crabgrass Grows by Itself

WHEN we first moved to the country, I thought that grass grew automatically everywhere cement wasn't. I took for granted magnificent trees, wide views and rolling green meadows that fairly spouted with springs and natural wells. And I assumed all these things would look unfailingly glorious all year long.

I know better now. I know, for example, that only after you have seeded a lawn with gold does that green stuff come up. I have learned that grass isn't simply *grass* but one of a million or so forms of vegetation which will or will not grow in sun, or in shade, or near water or away from it. I understand that trees must be pruned, sprayed and fed. I realize that a good compost heap is worth its weight in flowers, and I accept the fact (but don't understand why) that you buy manure by the yard. I've seen winter gardens turn grey and ugly for weeks; I've learned that for the sake of next year's blooms, this year's tulip leaves must be left standing to wither away by themselves. And I know that views don't "just grow" as often as they are made by ingenious professional people like Alice Orme Smith.

We first met Miss Smith when we lived on Black Rock Turnpike during the Second World War. The house we bought had not much to recommend it in the way of architectural beauty. And its sole asset where landscaping was concerned was a great round oak, perfectly symmetrical, that grew in the center of the driveway. It was such a magnificent tree that it once became the hero of a Moss Hart story, or rather a story in which Moss and the tree co-starred. Moss was wild about trees; with a lavishly haphazard hand, he'd spent a fortune planting them all over his Bucks County farm only to have them grow up all wrong—blocking out views he liked and pointing up things he had actually meant to hide. Undaunted, he had them all torn up and started over. Just about this time Moss came up to Connecticut to spend a weekend with Edna Ferber, and they drove over to see us.

Moss was stunned at the sight of the oak. "Oh," I said, "we felt the driveway needed a focal point, and so we moved it in." Since the roots of the tree spread roughly fifty feet in all directions, I was sure he would know I was joking, but he blanched visibly, then fired all sorts of questions (who had moved it? how big a ball of earth had it carried with it?). We parried them for an hour, then finally had to confess that the tree had established residence in that spot some three hundred years before we had arrived in Connecticut. Moss wasn't much amused, but he forgave us—for the tree's sake, I think.

Even with the help of the oak, there wasn't much that Miss Smith could do for the Turnpike house. She did plant a groundcover of pachysandra under the tree, and she replaced the hideous so-called garden (made uglier by a very ungraceful stone fountain) with a quite pretty irregular oval of planting. But that was just about all there was room for. And besides, since we knew this would not be our permanent home, we didn't want to invest huge sums in landscaping.

Creating Views

It was not until we bought Rockmeadow that Miss Smith had a chance to demonstrate her true talent. Although she rarely takes on a remodeling job (like most fine dressmakers, she would much rather start from scratch than make alterations), she agreed to help us. And in a very short time I learned to trust her entirely. When she says, "I see a view there," you can count on it—there will be a view there, no matter how dense the forest looks at present. At times she may sound vague ("and there will be . . . yes . . . ," she murmurs with a great sweep of her arm), but *she* knows exactly what she means. The picture in her mind is precise to the last detail; it is your vision that is limited. At Rockmeadow one afternoon we were talking plans when she made one of those large, mystic gestures: "I see a pond . . . there," she declared. And Dick looked dubious immediately; he made it clear that he wanted no five-year plans; if there was to be a pond, it would have to be done right then. It sounded like much too vast a project, but, quietly, Miss Smith assured us she could do it. She went to work, obtained the necessary permits, consulted state engineers, who, in Connecticut, offer free counseling on such technical matters as how big a dam will be needed, where it should be placed and what chemicals should be used to control algae without harming the wildlife in or around the water. Next spring we had our pond, and it was the perfect finishing touch Miss Smith had promised it would be.

Several things appeal to me about the way she works. First, she prefers to "open up vistas" rather than enclose spaces. Second, no detail is too small to be worthy of her attention (it was she who found the perfect place—sheltered, yet accessible to both the house and outdoors—to stack firewood in the garage). And finally, her approach has remained fresh and full of enthusiasm through all the years we've known her. Contemporary architecture pleases her; so does sculpture in a garden (she loves the Manzu). Once when a prickly specimen put me off, she offered as a substitute "something nice you can pat"; to her, plants are living, exciting things to be treated with care and respect; yet she doesn't give you the threatened sense that she and the landscaping are about to take over. She never works according to a set formula. She has always made us feel that she is planning for us, for our particular house, with the things and shapes we like best.

When it comes to remembering personal idiosyncrasies (like my dislike for orange flowers), she is a marvel. Where I am concerned, she has guessed wrong only once. We were discussing the new house when she implied we might like some topiary trees. I hastened to assure her that we didn't want any, thank you. Trees trimmed like poodles and peacocks didn't fit with my idea of a maintenance-free garden; not only would I much rather look at sculpture, but it doesn't have to be clipped. However, on almost everything else we have seen eye to eye in spite of my encyclopedic ignorance about growing things. (Before her arrival, the closest I'd come to gardening was "large plant in four letters" in the Sunday crossword puzzles.)

Miss Smith started work before Mike's men so much as turned a spade. It was she who showed us how we could take advantage of the highest point in the land, improve the view and save some of our most beautiful trees by simply shifting the house about seventy-five feet north of the spot where John and Oliver had placed it.

Paul Heetmann, our gardener, got an early start, too. By fall he had not only put in hyacinth and tulip bulbs in hopes we would have them for the following spring, but had transplanted several shrubs from Rockmeadow, not to their final places but to spots where they could safely be heeled in on the new property. With the new owner's permission, and being careful not to take anything that would leave a hole, we moved some rhododendron, some azaleas and a few dogwood trees which we had planted in a back meadow. There was also an espaliered evergreen which Paul had trained against the Rockmeadow greenhouse and which the new owner could not use. We took our fuchsia and geranium standards, some slips of pachysandra and, of course, Paul's patiently-tended compost heap—an item so important that we actually had it specifically mentioned in the bill of sale.

Miss Smith likes to start when work begins on the foundation of the house. Too often, she feels, people don't get around to calling in a landscape architect until everything else is done, at which point some of the knowledge that might have been most valuable to them —on siting, exposures, shapes of terraces and so on—is of absolutely no use. Or worse, in concentrating on building, they forget about planting entirely until it is too late and there's no money left to work with. Not consulting a landscape architect might sound like an economy, but it isn't—because the mistakes you can make on your own, without a Miss Smith to guide you, can be enormously costly.

The aim of a landscape architect is different from that of a building architect whose creation is complete when construction is done. Planting is only the start of a landscaping project; if its designer has been truly successful, his work will be much more beautiful ten years later when shrubs and flowers have had time to settle in. As Miss Smith says, it is never finished.

Without the experience that enables a professional to foresee how a garden will grow, amateur planners can go expensively astray. Focused on now, they often overplant so drastically that the flourishing specimens they have bought have no room to breathe or expand. Their growth occurs so gradually that one fails to notice when bushes whose proportions looked perfectly reasonable have shot up to block out a window's light and view. Among new customers at a nursery, there's an almost irresistible urge to buy a dozen of everything (because often the proprietor quotes his prices that way); and, though that may be a perfectly good way to order cans of tomatoes or even dining-room chairs, it is no way to deal with ornaments, which after all is what plants are.

Then there is the matter of care. It is the mistaken assumption of city types like me that if, for example, you have apple trees, you have apples—as simple as that. Nothing could be further from the truth. Apple trees must be pruned and sprayed and pampered. A farmer who wants a commercial crop sprays his orchard about twenty times a year. We had to have Rockmeadow's trees sprayed eight times even to get enough fruit for applesauce. In fact, as far as I have been able to learn, there is nothing this side of crabgrass that "just grows."

Unlike indoor plants and cut flowers, which can be moved at will, outdoor planting is permanent and must be schemed so that bloom follows bloom throughout the season. Because most shrubs are best transplanted when they are dormant, it is also easy to forget that the colors of flowering bushes planted next to each other should harmonize if they bloom at the same time. It's too late when, come spring, you discover to your horror that the azalea next to the purple rhododendron is salmon pink instead of white. Professionals like Miss Smith tag plants when they are in bloom in the nursery so that, although a particular specimen may not be moved for months, you get exactly the color you want.

Besides all this, plants have special qualities that take knowing. For example, under elms, or at least under ours at Rockmeadow, grass seems to thrive. On the other hand, at least one kind of maple makes soil so acid that no grass will grow anywhere near it. All growing things have their favorite climates, so that, no matter how glorious a calla lily looks in a California nursery's catalogue, it will not survive a move to New York.

An expert may also be able to suggest ways of planting or

using flowers—in baskets or raised beds or tubs, for instance, that might otherwise not have occurred to you. Our friends the Godowskys found that in their garden, which has quite a Japanese feeling, two dead trees, pruned and treated with a preservative, gave an almost sculptural feeling.

Skillfully handled, landscaping is a practical process as well as an aesthetic one. Of course, you want beautiful planting for its own sake. But if it is well planned, it will also show your house to its best advantage. It can point up a particularly striking view or mask one that's not so pretty. And in addition, it can be designed to minimize the cost and trouble of maintenance—a major consideration for us.

We were, of course, very fortunate in the property we had found. The curve of the land was gentle enough so that grading presented no problems, and a survey confirmed the fact that we wouldn't have to blast to put in our foundation. We were even blessed with our own layer of good topsoil. Still, we discovered that there was extensive work to be done before new plans or planting could begin.

We could never have bought or transplanted nursery trees the size of those already growing on our land. But most of them were being choked and crowded by underbrush that would have to be cleared out, and because of a blight that's quite serious in our part of the country, the elms, too, would have to come down. The old apple trees, though lovely, needed pruning and care. And, of course, nothing on the place had been fed in years. I can't argue with Miss Smith's dictum that a tree worth keeping is a tree worth feeding. But I never knew plant life could eat so much. The cost before we got anywhere near the fun of selecting our first new peony was a fairly staggering sum.

However, the time did come, and we started touring the nurseries with Miss Smith. The three of us seemed in perfect accord about what we thought would look best; without actually being conscious of it, we found ourselves thinking in terms of things quite different from those we had used at Rockmeadow. The shrubbery was much more contemporary, almost oriental, to complement the lines of the house. I fell in love with one tree I had never known existed. It was a weeping spruce—and magnificent. It looked almost like a piece of sculpture covered with evergreen boughs; and it carried me back to an old movie about World War I, *Shoulder Arms*, in which Charlie Chaplin was camouflaged as a tree. Even though "he" was expensive, for quite a while I set my heart on Charlie. But in the long run we found there was really no place in our planting scheme important enough to be worthy of him. If the trees we bought were beautiful and provided the shade we needed, rare exotic varieties weren't necessary. As long as I could have one shiny-leaved magnolia and a copper beach, I'd be satisfied.

Informality in Landscaping

Except for the croquet field with its automatic sprinkler system, there would be no manicured lawn. We decided on gravel rather than grass for the garden paths, and on borders of *fraises des bois* not only because they'd look pretty and give us delicious fruit, but because they'd eliminate trimming (our friends Jane Grant and Bill Harris suggested the idea and later sent us plants from their nursery, White Flower Farm, as a housewarming present). Keeping an informal feeling, we gave up the idea of rows of dogwood along the driveway and decided instead to set them here and there around the croquet field. We would have lots of espaliered trees because I love their look and because all of us felt they would be so especially right against the silvery walls of the house.

The pool was a most important area—from the point of view

of people both inside and outside the house. After all, any time we were not playing croquet, we would be sitting around the pool. Basically, my notion about placing plants around the terrace was to treat them almost like pieces of sculpture or furniture—setting tubs of geraniums on either side of the ladder into the pool, standards (geraniums or fuchsias) by the windows of Dick's room and others to balance them across the terrace by the storage-room wall. There would be large pots of daisies standing on the low stone walls and a pair of small evergreen trees—*Chamaecyparis obtusa*, Miss Smith calls them—in very simple white tubs. (I hope to add bonsai trees later.) Miss Smith vetoed my idea of growing herbs between the flagstones of the terrace as impractical, but she liked the idea—which we took from the Museum of Modern Art's garden—of leaving planting holes for low shrubs.

It is quite usual for a landscape architect to submit drawings of the things he plans to do. But after twenty-five years with Miss Smith, we didn't feel these were necessary. So, once we visualized the same sort of thing, she continued her rounds unescorted. She knew every nurseryman and his stock, and everyone she used was expert. But finding the right thing for the right spot can consume enormous amounts of time and energy, especially in these days when good nurseries and really beautiful specimen plants are becoming increasingly rare and costly.

For weeks we might not see her, but we could see the results of her work. She found two glorious laurels for the corners of the front courtyard and some particularly graceful upright yews (to me, they look very like cypress trees) to screen the sunken garbage cans in the service yard. Espaliered pear and fig trees appeared along with some locust trees, birches, spruce and hemlocks. There were to be two white wistarias against the garage wall and hanging baskets of fuchsia outside the windows on either side of the front door.

Around the pool and in front of the house, outdoor lighting would add a subtle drama to the planting at night. In addition to the railway lamp and the lights above the doors, lights on either side of the entrance would bathe the hanging baskets. Ground lights that will eventually be masked by shrubs have been set on the meadow side of the courtyard and on the croquet-field side of the front wall and aimed at the tops of the trees. In the pool area a grill-covered light set in the flagstones bathes the Manzu; others, camouflaged by ground-cover, play on the tops of the dogwood and the birch. And pool lights make the water look just as blue at night as it does in the daytime, which is really quite extraordinary when you consider that the pool itself is painted white.

Miss Smith planned several kinds of ground-cover, myrtle and pachysandra mostly, and a grouping of evergreens that would act as a screen between the main road and the house. Great Brobdingnagian steppingstones leading from the terrace outside Dick's bedroom would eventually have thyme and low oriental-looking yews planted around them. Miss Smith had created what John calls a forced perspective at the bottom of the meadow by persuading the men at the wildlife preserve to let her take down one tree here and another there so that the eye would be led just where she wanted it to go.

Every once in a while she would materialize, trailing wisps of flowers she thought we might like; one day she brought rose blooms for us to choose from (we decided on white because of the walls and also because it would not clash with the vivid geraniums and the fuchsia pinks). And another time, from the depths of her large bag, she produced a collection of plastic pill bottles filled with samples of stone chips for the surface of the driveway. Sometimes she would surprise us with plants she thought would do well for us that she had found while thinning another client's garden. Then she'd be off again.

Meanwhile more surprises were being turned up from quite another source: the foundation digging had unearthed a number of spectacular boulders, one especially imposing example of which intrigued us for a while. Dick thought perhaps we could install it in the front field and name this house for the one we'd left behind. But I felt this would be a mistake, since this wasn't to be a second Rockmeadow and we didn't really want to suggest that it was. Our next idea was to place the rock, half buried, near the end of the croquet field as a kind of combination natural hazard and possible spectators' perch. Then we realized that a ball driven hard against it might split or ricochet dangerously, and, besides, the rock would be a monumental nuisance to mow around. So, in the end, it was buried again.

Designing the Driveway

As I say, our faith in Miss Smith was complete. But if it hadn't been, one incident that took place toward the end of the building would have established it for sure. It had to do with the placing of the driveway. Oliver Lundquist felt that it should cut gently across the front field and double back on itself just before it reached the house. John rather agreed with Oliver; I think they both felt this longer drive would produce a desirable illusion of greater distance from the road. (A pretentious house we once rented on Long Island had a driveway so tortured with curves that, although the distance between the house and the highway was actually quite short, you felt you had driven miles to reach the front door.) But Miss Smith was adamant. She felt that the big unbroken meadow made an important contribution. To her, the square shapes of the house and the meadow were so clearly related that cutting across the field would destroy something very precious. The more I pictured the alternative she suggested—that we bring the road in along the north edge of the property, then turn it south past the service yard and into the front court—the more reasonable it seemed. Not only would the field be saved, but by detouring service trucks before they reached the bedroom wing, we would do a great deal to preserve our country peace.

Having lived with it now, I can testify that it has worked just as she said it would. Instead of being propelled directly toward the front door of the house, you are led up to it by stages, past a series of pleasant surprises, which is just what architects try to achieve. A subtle planting line directs your eye toward the great oak on the left of the driveway, and in the front courtyard granite bollards serve both to give scale to the house and to indicate the turnabout.

Not long ago a friend, seeing the house for the first time, made us very happy by saying, "This house seems to welcome you with open arms." Basically, of course, this grows from the beauty of John's design for the courtyard. But Miss Smith, through her genius with growing things, has added a very special warmth.

CHAPTER EIGHT

Elegance without Finger Bowls

THE title of this chapter takes me back four years to a little game that Dick and I and many of our friends used to play. It was called "Trying to Think of a Name for Dorothy's Book." And when Mary came up with the idea that *My Favorite Things* would cover the subject pretty well, she won hands down. However, before *MFT* came along, there had been other title contenders. "How to Live Elegant" was the one we had most fun with, although we knew it was really too tongue-in-cheek to be right. "Elegance Without Finger Bowls" was another, and I'm glad now that it lost the contest. It suits the new house so much better.

Our first party there was perhaps the most informal we have ever given. In the tileless, rugless living room, the beer flowed like champagne, and there wasn't a slice of pâté or a cucumber sandwich in sight. The buffet—three boards on saw-horses—groaned with grinders, salads, smoked fish, cheeses, sausages and great hearty stacks of bread. And most of our sixty guests wore overalls. It was our roof-tree party.

Late in the spring of 1966, on one of our weekly visits, I had spied a strange skeleton of a tree high on the ridge of the newly finished slate roof. There were a few wrinkled oranges tied to its pitiful bones, and the whole thing conjured up vague recollections of an old custom having to do with the closing-in of a house. Seeing where I was looking, Mike asked if I knew what the "roof tree" meant. I was ready to launch a vague cultured guess when he answered his own question:

"It means a party," he said.

It did indeed. The tradition goes back to the earliest days of building when every time a neighbor needed a new house or barn or shed, the whole town pitched in. When the highest point of the building was reached, the tree was installed and all hands took time out for a party at which the new owner played host.

I didn't know how much of what to buy for sixty men, all hungry from a day's work. But Jimmy Mercurio, our market man, came to the rescue. He had, it seemed, catered a dozen celebrations like ours. Beer and delicatessen, he assured me, were just what the guests wanted—as long as there was plenty of both. And he took over from there.

Friday, June 3rd, dawned bright and balmy; and by a little after three, plumbers and painters, carpenters and electricians, stonemasons and steamfitters, the engineers, John and Oliver and Miss Smith had all gathered. The weather was so beautiful that the photographer Ezra Stoller was able to take lots of pictures—first, of all of us at ground level with a symbolic roof tree in full leaf, then of Mike and a few of his regulars who clambered onto the roof to pose with the real thing. Roger, our mascot, romped about being everybody's friend (everybody was feeding him); and the men, proud of the house and the work they had done, milled around wishing us well. We thanked them, meaning every word, and as those first guests drove off, I could hardly wait for the day when others would be arriving.

From the beginning, I looked forward to entertaining in a more informal way in the new house. Obviously, this meant important changes in the way meals were prepared and served. We took the first big step in the planning stage when we decided not to have a separate room for dining, but to use part of the living room instead. The problem was to find a graceful way to set and clear the table. Folding doors near the pantry gave us a small area out of sight in which tables could be set before the meal. But the pass-through in the wall between the pantry and the living room provided the most important part of our answer.

When I have help, the food and wine are placed on the buffet counter where things can be kept hot in chafing dishes or on the built-in electrically-heated tray; then the doors on the pantry side are closed, the ones in the living room are opened and guests can serve themselves. When I do the cooking and serving myself, the doors on both sides are left open to simplify things. And in either case, once the meal is over, everything is put back on the buffet, the living-room doors are closed and clearing away is done from the pantry side.

With this sort of buffet arrangement, we can eliminate formal service and the kind of table settings that call for place plates and finger bowls, which have always seemed inappropriate in the country. The table, or tables (each one seats only six), are set with linens, flatware, butter plates, salt, pepper, cigarettes and ashtrays. And everything else—glasses, plates, food and wine—is arranged on the serving counter. We can handle the changing of courses in either of two ways. The tables can be cleared onto the buffet counter, in which case the doors on the living-room side are closed, and dessert and coffee are brought in on a two-tiered cart (this way, we can even move to another part of the room if we like). Or, the cart is used for table clearing while, opening the pantry doors only partway,

Inez removes the main-course serving dishes and sets out the dessert things.

Behind the scenes, the kitchen has turned out to be not only handsome but a wonderful place in which to work. Even with hindsight, if I were planning it now, I would not change anything about its basic arrangement. The appliance and work areas are exactly where they should be to function with greatest efficiency. A few pieces of equipment have not, in practice, quite lived up to their advertising copy, and they have been something of a disappointment. But at least one has been a joy. Unquestionably, the appliance that has made the greatest change in my cooking habits is the vertical freezer that stands next to the kitchen refrigerator.

Freezers have come a long way since the days of World War II when, to save money and ration points, we went halves with a neighbor to buy a steer (a bum steer it turned out to be—very few steaks and mostly ground meat). Because Rockmeadow's freezer was in the basement, we thought of it as a storage place where food could be kept for emergencies. We used it infrequently and grudgingly. But now that the freezer is so accessible, all that has changed. It has become an active part of my cooking life.

It is a common misconception that food can't be as good after it has been frozen as before. True, only pastry dough is actually improved by freezing, but food frozen promptly and quickly (both promptness and fast freezing are very important) will retain the freshness it had at the time of freezing. And it is a pleasant feeling to have a stock of your own home cooking ready to serve at short notice.

I've learned to use the freezer in a dozen ways. Leftover sauces, for instance, can be frozen in ice-cube trays, then separated and stored in plastic bags. That way they can be used in small amounts as you need them—perhaps a couple of cubes of hollandaise to put on some leaf spinach or to enrich a sauce you are making.

A look at the list of the freezer's contents not only suggests possibilities, it even encourages me to become creative and invent new dishes from what I have on hand. One rainy morning when Dick and I were alone, we decided not to drive the ten miles to and from the fish market but to see what could be rustled up without leaving the kitchen. I came up with all kinds of things from the freezer: some crabmeat, a bit of sauce left over from a poached chicken, a package of spinach and a package of frozen crêpes I had bought to try out. In my reserve of canned goods, I found French mushrooms in cream. I heated the crabmeat and mushrooms together, added the sauce from the freezer, some sherry and a bit of salt and pepper. Then I filled the thawed pancakes with some of the mixture, rolled them, put them in a baking dish and into the oven just long enough to heat them. I served the rest of the crabmeat mixture as a sauce and sprinkled some ground nutmeg on the spinach just before serving it. It was a very good lunch indeed.

I try to be careful about marking containers and packages with tape and keeping the list of the freezer's contents up to date. It's a chore that is, unfortunately, easy to forget, but it is essential. I find it helps to list foods by classifications: soups, fish and seafood, poultry, meats, breads, fruits, vegetables and desserts. And I make note of quantities—information that is especially useful when it comes to leftovers. "Four to six servings" tells you what you need to know.

When I was doing the cooking, I found that I liked to do as much as possible on Mondays. This usually meant making some soups, preparing tart shells, baking a chocolate or ginger roll, perhaps making some sherbet or an ice-cream bombe and freezing it in a mold. Often I would prepare a beef or veal or lamb casserole so that when the weekend arrived, I would not have so much to do.

Although my chief pleasure comes from the great flexibility the freezer makes possible, it also cuts down the drudgery of cooking (making twice the quantity you need and freezing half means only one set of pots to scour). It's nice to know that the intelligent use of a freezer can be economical, too. Many things that would have gone to waste otherwise are now saved and used; and it is possible to lay in a supply of reserves by taking advantage of "specials" in the market. I have found it is even worth the few seconds it takes to freeze very small amounts; enough for one serving can be very welcome on a busy day when you are alone.

I try to freeze things in quantities that are useful for different occasions. Whether two-, four- or eight-portion packages are most helpful depends on both the size of your family and the kind of meal at which you plan to use them. I freeze many foods in small containers so that I won't have to thaw more than we need when Dick and I are alone. When there are more of us, I can always take out two or more packages. Things I plan to serve to guests—sherbet or a chocolate roll, for instance—I freeze in larger quantities. Quite often I soften ice cream or water ice and pack it into molds so that instead of a formless mass or dull scoops, I have something that looks special.

I've found that a little leisure invested in preparations can pay huge dividends when I'm expecting guests and pressed for time. At Middy Darrow's suggestion, I now mix butter with flour or tarragon, lemon or parsley, and freeze small amounts in individually labeled packages whenever I have time. Parsley or dill or chives from the garden, chopped and frozen in small containers, not only save time and trouble, but add fresh flavor that's hard to come by when they are not in season. Even whipped cream can be frozen: small dabs placed on a sheet of paper until they freeze can then be stored in a plastic container; they won't stick together, and they will thaw in ten or fifteen minutes.

In addition to things you make at home, there are, of course, excellent commercial products that are not only delicious but great

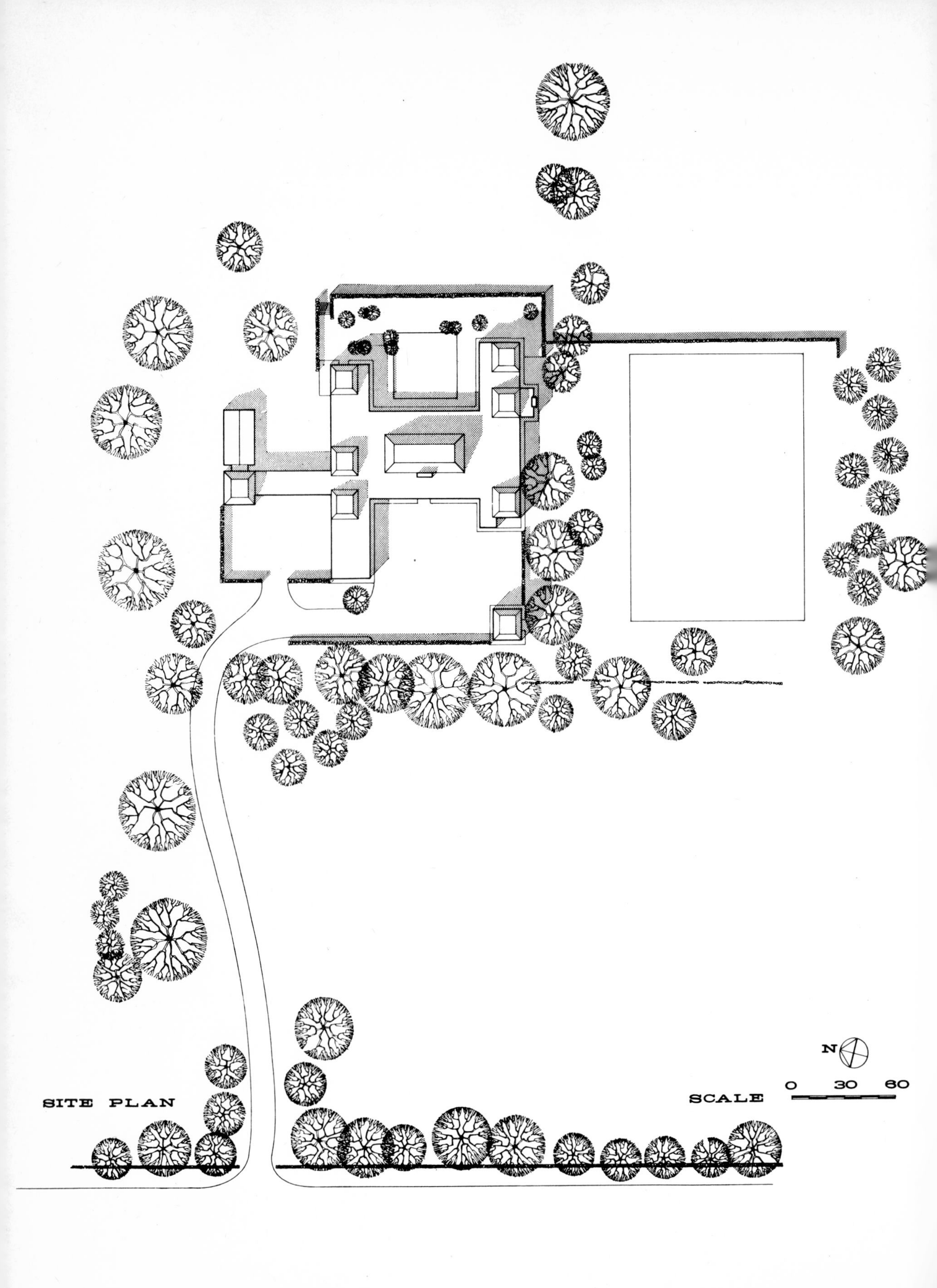
SITE PLAN
SCALE
0 30 60
N

time-savers. We use a great many frozen vegetables because, as a rule, they seem tenderer and smaller than those that are available in the market. Frozen tiny young peas and baby lima beans are just as I like them best. And foods frozen close to the place where they are grown retain a fresh flavor that's often missing in so-called "fresh" vegetables after they have been shipped and stored. Among frozen fruits, raspberries are excellent for making sauces, and the strawberries do beautifully in a soufflé or a mousse.

To supplement foods in the freezer, I keep a varied supply of canned goods. When you want to invite guests to stay for lunch or dinner on the spur of the moment, it is comforting to know that you can concoct a very good first course of canned artichoke bottoms filled with mushrooms (the kind that are packed in brine) and sprinkled with French dressing. Starting with a can of minced clams, pasta (elbow macaroni, spaghetti or linguini) and a nice chunk of Parmesan cheese (ungrated, it keeps for months in the refrigerator and tastes much better than the ready-grated kind), you can put together a delicious dish. Even canned truffles needn't be prohibitively expensive when you know the trick of using one truffle and covering the rest with Madeira to preserve them. And many canned soups are first-rate—especially when you combine them or add some herbs or wine. For dessert emergencies, I usually keep one or two cans of lichee nuts and some crystallized ginger—two very different Chinese delicacies that can be used many ways (on vanilla ice cream, for example). Mixed with summer fruits, the lichee nuts add a subtle flavor that intrigues people because they don't recognize it immediately.

They say a famous chef once divided the process of learning to cook into three stages. In the first, he said, the cook is timid, follows directions precisely and gets results that are, barring errors, as good as the recipe she uses. In the second stage, she makes no errors; and in the third, she makes mistakes, but she has learned how to correct them. I think there is a fourth stage when, after mastering the basic techniques of making soups or sauces or pastry, she creates her own variations.

Until they have had a good deal of experience, many women tend to stick to recipes slavishly. But recipes themselves can seldom be entirely exact. How large is a bunch of leeks or a medium-sized onion, for instance? What about variations in the size of eggs and in the ability of even the finest ovens to attain and maintain perfectly the exact temperature called for?

So don't necessarily be bound by printed recipes. By using what you have on hand or what is readily available, by making intelligent substitutions, by thinking about different ways of serving what are unappetizingly referred to as "leftovers," you can discover the pleasure of inventing your own dishes. And keeping these principles in mind will compound your interest.

Many things about cooking are highly personal. Matters of seasoning, for example, have to be decided according to your own and your family's tastes. To use herbs effectively, you should have more than a reading or sniffing acquaintance with a number of them. Learn what they actually taste like so that you will know which ones are generally used to bring out the flavors of specific foods, and so that you can experiment with your own new combinations.

Over the years, I've discovered, or developed a few cooking idiosyncrasies of my own. When I was the cook last summer, I found I used relatively little cream and milk and almost no heavy cream; even in soups I use light cream or creamy milk. This is partly because we like foods that are not too rich, but also because it's simply more considerate in these days when almost everyone is careful about diet. We don't deep-fry, partly for the sake of digestibility, but also because all that crackling fat scares me. I prefer a light salad oil to olive oil, which, to me, has a stronger, heavier flavor. I use cornstarch, which gives a lovely translucent sheen, instead of flour to give substance to dark sauces. I have an extravagant tendency to use chicken, beef or fish stock in place of water whenever possible. And since neither Dick nor I like garlic, you'll find that my recipes call for shallots instead.

While it is almost a cliché to say that hot foods should be served hot, I find that cold meats and fish are often served so rigidly cold that much of their flavor is lost. I like to serve them at room temperature or, if they are glazed with aspic, only just cold enough to prevent the aspic from melting.

I have my own pet time-savers, too. Though I know that some gourmets consider it a crime, I buy prepared mayonnaise. And in spite of my mother's good example (she used to order a veal knuckle, a shin bone, the shank and marrow bones and start stock from "hello-hello"), the chicken and beef stocks we use in sauces and soups are also bought ready-made. However, the chicken soup we serve is made at home; and when we have duck or turkey, I like soup made from the carcasses and meat that is left.

The menus and recipes that will follow at the end of this chapter have been adapted for informal entertaining. Their purpose is to simplify life. So I have tried to keep the recipes uncomplicated and easy to prepare. They are all dishes we have enjoyed at home. But in things that call for tart shells or pastry dough, I have started from scratch in the old-fashioned way although I know that there are many good mixes on the market. If you have favorites, use them. I hope you'll take advantage of all the short-cuts that work for you whenever, wherever you can.

As often as possible, I have tried to suggest ways of using leftovers, but since no two women are ever faced with exactly the same ones, this is a challenge that, basically, has to be left to your own imagination. You may come up with something original that is far better than any recipe I could give.

I have suggested crisp, crusted breads—French and Italian and others—because I don't happen to like soft rolls or plain white bread. I like croissants and popovers if they are well-made and light. I like good old-fashioned rye bread with caraway seeds, pumpernickel with certain dishes (smoked salmon, for example), sesame crackers and bread sticks and, occasionally, pappadums. It is important to vary the breads you serve, which, again, will depend on the ones you like best.

I've been deliberately vague when it comes to wines. The right choice is a matter of menu and budget. But what makes the greatest difference is your own knowledge of what you and your husband and guests like best. And that, of course, makes your menus personal. The ones that follow are merely suggestions.

Menus and Recipes

(Each menu is followed by recipes of starred item or items.)

MENU 1

Oyster Stew
Popovers — Cold Ham Mousse* — Verdicchio
Salade Niçoise
Lemon Sherbet, Raspberry Sauce

There are many variations of salade niçoise. My version includes black olives, tuna fish, tomatoes, celery and capers to be added to the basic string beans and sliced potatoes. The dressing should be a classic one of oil, vinegar, salt and pepper. Chopped chervil and tarragon sprinkled over the salad bring out all the flavors.

I make the raspberry sauce by saving the juice from the frozen berries and straining it to remove the seeds. Add a little sugar and some Kirsch. The sauce is lovely when it is made with strawberry juice, too.

HAM MOUSSE

(8–10 Servings)

2 cups boiled ham, cut up
1 teaspoon Dijon mustard
Cayenne
¼ teaspoon salt
1 tablespoon gelatin
1 cup heavy cream, whipped
½ cup boiling water
1 tablespoon cold water
1 drop red food coloring
Truffles (optional)
Parsley

Grind 2 cups boiled ham in blender; add 1 teaspoon Dijon mustard, dash of cayenne and ¼ teaspoon salt. In mixing bowl, soften 1 tablespoon gelatin in 1 tablespoon cold water; add ½ cup boiling water. Add ham mixture to liquid. Whip 1 cup heavy cream; color faintly with 1 drop red food coloring. Fold whipped cream into ham and pour mousse into greased loaf pan (or other greased mold) and refrigerate for 2 hours or until set. Unmold onto a chilled platter and garnish with chopped truffles and parsley.

MENU 2

Cheese Soufflé
Filets of Sole Maison*
French Bread — Purée of Peas — Soave
Asparagus Vinaigrette
Mixed Compote of Fruit
Oatmeal Cookies*

Be sure your guests are ready for the soufflé before it is ready for them. If you have any leftover vegetables, purée them in a blender with the peas. You'll end up with a whole new flavor. This can also be done from scratch, of course, combining such vegetables as broccoli, lima beans, tomatoes, etc.

FILETS OF SOLE MAISON

(8–10 Servings)

16 filets of sole
Juice of 2 lemons

1¼ cups dry white wine
8 tablespoons cold water
1 teaspoon salt
10 whole black peppercorns
4 small bay leaves
1 pound mushrooms
2 tablespoons lemon juice
5 tablespoons butter
1 pound cooked shrimp

Preheat oven to 350°

Wash 16 filets of sole in cold water and juice of 2 lemons. Pat dry. Butter 1 large or 2 smaller shallow baking dishes, roll up each filet and arrange in a row down center of dish. Cover with 1¼ cups dry white wine, 8 tablespoons cold water, 1 teaspoon salt, 10 whole black peppercorns and 4 small bay leaves. Put dish over asbestos mats or flame tamers on top of range over moderate heat and bring liquid to a boil. Turn down heat and simmer for 2 minutes, basting while fish is cooking. Strain off most of liquid and reserve. Remove bay leaves and peppercorns. Bake in preheated 350° oven for 12–15 minutes, basting once or twice. Meanwhile, wash, stem and slice 1 pound mushrooms. Sprinkle with 2 tablespoons lemon juice and sauté them for about 3 minutes in 5 tablespoons butter. Add mushroom liquid to already reserved fish liquid.

SAUCE

6 tablespoons butter
8 tablespoons flour
2 cups milk, heated
¼ cup dry white wine

½ cup clam juice
Fish and mushroom liquid
1 teaspoon salt
½ teaspoon white pepper

Melt 6 tablespoons butter, add 8 tablespoons flour and cook for about 3 minutes over low heat but do not brown. Heat milk and add to butter-flour mixture after removing it from heat. Stir with wooden spoon until smooth and well blended. Replace over low heat and, stirring constantly, add ¼ cup dry white wine, ½ cup clam juice and reserve liquid (from fish and mushrooms); strain into top part of 1 large double boiler (or 2 smaller ones). Season with 1 teaspoon salt and ½ teaspoon white pepper, or to taste. Add 1 pound cooked shrimp and heat them thoroughly in sauce. Add 1 pound cooked mushrooms just before serving. Pour sauce with shrimp and mushrooms over filets and serve.

OATMEAL COOKIES

(*5 dozen*)

¼ pound butter (1 bar)
½ cup sugar
1 cup flour
½ teaspoon salt
½ teaspoon baking powder
¼ cup light cream
¼ cup dark Karo syrup
1½ cups oatmeal
1 teaspoon vanilla extract

Preheat oven to 400°

Cream ¼ pound butter with ½ cup sugar. Sift together 1 cup flour, ½ teaspoon salt, ½ teaspoon baking powder and add gradually to mixture. Pour in ¼ cup light cream and ¼ cup dark Karo syrup, blending thoroughly. Add 1½ cups oatmeal all at once, 1 teaspoon vanilla extract and blend carefully. Since this batter spreads in baking, drop only *½ teaspoonfuls*, 2 inches apart, on well-greased cookie sheet. Bake at 400° for 4–5 minutes.

MENU 3

Spring Soup*
Croissants — Lamb Curry in Crèpes* — Tavel
Chutney
Sliced Tomatoes with Basil and French Dressing
Sour Cherry Tart

As an alternative, use a combination of chicken and lobster in the crèpes with curry sauce. Or, try substituting strudel dough (which can be bought commercially and kept in the refrigerator for weeks or in the freezer for months) for the crèpes. Fresh basil is particularly delicious on raw sliced tomatoes.

SPRING SOUP

(*6–8 Servings*)

2 bunches scallions, trimmed and chopped
2 large carrots, sliced thin
¼ pound butter (1 bar)
½ pound fresh or frozen asparagus, cut into ½-inch pieces

2 cups peas
6 cups strong chicken stock

Sauté 2 bunches trimmed and chopped scallions and 2 thinly sliced carrots in ¼ pound butter over a low flame for 2–3 minutes. Add ½ pound asparagus and 2 cups peas and sauté 3–4 minutes more. Add 6 cups strong chicken stock; bring to a boil, lower heat and simmer for ½ hour or until vegetables are tender (not mushy). Serve hot. Soup may be frozen if desired.

LAMB CURRY IN CRÊPES

(8–10 Servings)

CRÊPES

¼ pound plus 1 tablespoon butter (1 bar and 1 tablespoon)
4 large eggs
¼ teaspoon salt
1½ cups club soda (1½ 8-ounce bottles)
1½ cups flour

Clarify ¼ pound plus 1 tablespoon butter and keep warm in top half of double boiler. In an electric blender, put 4 eggs, ¼ teaspoon salt, 1½ cups club soda and 1½ cups flour. Blend until smooth. Heat a 5-inch crêpe pan (or small frying pan) and brush with clarified butter. Pour 2 tablespoons batter onto center of pan and tilt, allowing batter to spread over entire pan. Cook crêpes quickly on both sides. Repeat process until all batter has been used. Keep crêpes warm while making lamb curry.

LAMB CURRY

3 pounds stewing lamb
1 quart beef stock
1 carrot, peeled
1 medium onion, peeled
4 sprigs parsley
1 tablespoon salt

Remove fat from 3 pounds stewing lamb and cut meat into 1-inch pieces. Cover with 1 quart beef stock. Add 1 peeled carrot, 1 peeled onion, 4 sprigs parsley and 1 tablespoon salt and bring to a boil. Lower heat and simmer for 1 hour, skimming every 15 minutes. Drain and reserve meat.

CURRY SAUCE

4 medium apples, peeled, cored and chopped
2 large white onions, peeled and chopped
6 stalks celery, chopped
¼ pound butter (1 bar)
2 tablespoons butter, melted
¼ cup flour
¼ cup curry powder
4 cups chicken stock, heated
½ cup light cream

In a large pot, melt ¼ pound butter. Add 4 chopped apples, 2 chopped onions, 6 chopped celery stalks and cook for 10–15 minutes or until soft. Blend 2 tablespoons melted butter with ¼ cup flour and ¼ cup curry powder; add to apple-onion-celery mixture and cook for 3–5 minutes, stirring constantly. Add 4 cups hot chicken stock and simmer over low heat for 30 minutes, stirring occasionally. Cool slightly and pour into blender. Blend until smooth. Pour sauce back into pot; add ½ cup light cream and stir well. Add cooked lamb and cook just long enough to re-heat meat and sauce. Fill crèpes with mixture; roll up and arrange on warm serving dish. Pour remaining sauce over all and serve with chutney.

MENU 4

Jellied Madrilène
Butterfly Steaks
Italian Bread — Spinach-and-Cheese Pie* — Red Burgundy
Mixed Green Salad
Strawberry Mousse*

Butterfly steaks are minute steaks that have been split but not completely severed. They should be grilled, of course; they cook very fast because they are so thin. Serve them with lemon-and-tarragon butter. The Spinach-and-Cheese Pie can be made with strudel dough or with phyllo, the Greek pastry dough. (Both are available commercially.) It is tricky because you must work quickly with the dough. But it can be made in the morning and re-heated, if necessary, at the time of serving.

SPINACH-AND-CHEESE PIE

(8–10 Servings)

4 10-ounce packages frozen chopped spinach
2 medium onions, chopped
⅓ cup oil

1½ teaspoons dried dill weed
½ teaspoon salt
¼ teaspoon pepper
¾ pound feta cheese, crumbled
20 phyllo pastry leaves (¾ pound)
½ pound butter, melted (2 bars)

Preheat oven to 350°

Cook 4 10-ounce packages frozen chopped spinach according to directions on package and drain thoroughly. Heat ⅓ cup oil and sauté 2 chopped onions until translucent. Stir in cooked spinach, 1½ teaspoons dried dill weed, ½ teaspoon salt and ¼ teaspoon pepper. Add ¾ pound crumbled feta cheese and toss lightly with spinach mixture. Grease a 13 x 9 x 2-inch oven-proof serving dish with some of the melted butter. (Since phyllo requires fast handling to prevent dough from crumbling, have all ingredients ready. It helps to put phyllo leaves on damp towel while working with them, but they can be patched if necessary. Phyllo dough may be bought at any Greek bakery.) Spread 10 phyllo leaves in baking dish, brushing each leaf lightly and quickly with melted butter. Add spinach-and-cheese mixture, spreading it evenly over the leaves. Top with 10 more phyllo leaves, again brushing each leaf lightly and quickly with melted butter. With a sharp knife, cut diagonally into portions. Brush top leaf with melted butter. Bake at 350° for 35–45 minutes or until pie is golden brown. Serve at room temperature.

STRAWBERRY MOUSSE

(6–8 Servings)

1 cup strawberries (1 10-ounce package, frozen)
4 teaspoons gelatin (1 envelope plus 1 teaspoon)
2 cups heavy cream, stiffly whipped

½ cup confectioner's sugar
1 teaspoon vanilla extract

Thaw contents of 1 package frozen strawberries; drain and reserve juice (1 cup). Soften 4 teaspoons gelatin in 1 cup strawberry juice and set aside. Whip 2 cups heavy cream until stiff and fold ½ cup confectioner's sugar and 1 teaspoon vanilla extract into whipped cream. Heat strawberry juice with gelatin until gelatin is completely dissolved; cool. Blend with strawberries and fold into whipped-cream mixture. Pour into lightly buttered 1-quart mold and refrigerate for 2 hours or until set. Unmold onto chilled serving dish. (Do not freeze.)

MENU 5

Shrimp Cocktail, Mayonnaise Maison*
Rye Bread — Pot Roast — Beer
Potato Pancakes
Broccoli, Hollandaise Sauce
Lemon Chiffon Pie*

Pot-roast-and-potato-pancakes seem like one word to me—so perfectly are they matched. How about some dill pickles to go with the main course?

COOKED SHRIMP

(for 8 shrimp cocktails)

1½ quarts water
2 cups dry white wine

2 tablespoons caraway seeds
2 teaspoons Lowry's seasoned salt
1 tablespoon dried tarragon (or 4 tablespoons fresh tarragon)
4 white onions, cut up
10 sprigs parsley
10 stalks celery, cut up (tops included)
2 teaspoons whole black peppercorns
2 pounds medium or large shrimp

In a large kettle, combine 1½ quarts water, 2 cups dry white wine, 2 tablespoons caraway seeds, 2 teaspoons Lowry's seasoned salt, 1 tablespoon dried tarragon, 4 white onions, cut up, 10 sprigs parsley, 10 stalks celery, cut up, and 2 teaspoons whole black peppercorns. Bring to a boil, lower heat and simmer for 40 minutes. Meanwhile, shell, devein and wash 2 pounds medium or large shrimp under cold water. Remove bouillon from heat and strain. Add shrimp to strained bouillon; bring to a boil, turn heat off and cover kettle. Leave shrimp in bouillon until shrimp have turned pink and are opaque. Remove shrimp and allow them to cool. Chill and serve with the following sauce:

MAYONNAISE MAISON

¼ cup brandy
1 cup mayonnaise
¼ cup fresh dill, finely chopped (or 1 tablespoon dried dill weed)

Blend together ¼ cup brandy, 1 cup mayonnaise and ¼ cup fresh dill, chopped fine, or 1 tablespoon dried dill weed.

LEMON CHIFFON PIE

(8–10 Servings)

TART SHELL (9-INCH)

1½ cups flour
1½ teaspoons granulated sugar
⅛ teaspoon salt
4 tablespoons chilled butter
4 tablespoons chilled vegetable shortening
3 tablespoons ice water

Preheat oven to 400°

Sift 1½ cups flour, 1½ teaspoons granulated sugar and ⅛ teaspoon salt into mixing bowl. Using a pastry blender or 2 knives, cut in 4 tablespoons chilled butter and 4 tablespoons chilled vegetable shortening until a very sandy mixture is obtained. Sprinkle dough with no more than 3 tablespoons ice water in order to gather it into a ball. (Handle as little as possible.) Wrap in towel and chill in refrigerator for at least 1 hour. Roll dough between 2 pieces of waxed paper, starting in center and rolling into a circle. When dough is a little larger than 9 inches, fold it in half and allow it to fall in place in a buttered 9-inch flan ring. Do not stretch dough. Press into ring and cut excess dough off with rolling pin. Chill or freeze until time to use. When baking unfilled tart shell, prick bottom of pastry with fork in several places; cover bottom with a round of waxed paper and spread uncooked rice on paper to keep dough in shape. Bake in preheated 400° oven until dough shrinks slightly from sides of pan and has begun to turn golden brown (about 15 minutes, depending on how cold dough was when it was put into oven). Remove from oven and from flan ring and let cool on cake rack before filling.

FILLING

1 teaspoon gelatin
¼ cup cold water
4 egg yolks, lightly beaten
1 cup and 1 tablespoon sugar
½ cup lemon juice
½ teaspoon salt
1 teaspoon lemon rind
4 egg whites, stiffly beaten
Cream of tartar
Almond slivers or grated chocolate

Soften 1 teaspoon gelatin in ¼ cup cold water. Beat 4 egg yolks lightly; add ½ cup sugar, ½ cup lemon juice, ½ teaspoon salt and cook in top half of double boiler, stirring constantly, until mixture coats metal spoon. Add 1 teaspoon lemon rind and the gelatin mixture and blend thoroughly. Remove from heat and allow to cool. Add pinch of cream of tartar to 4 egg whites and beat until they stand in peaks. When yolk mixture begins to thicken, fold in egg whites. Fold in remaining sugar (½ cup and 1 tablespoon). Fill baked tart shell and chill. Sprinkle top with roasted almond slivers or grated chocolate.

MENU 6

Black Bean Soup
French Bread   Endives in Ham, Cheese Sauce*   Pouilly-Fumé
String Beans, Almond Slivers
Baked Apple
Gingerbread*

I usually add a slice of lemon and some dry sherry to the soup. The endive dish is Belgian in origin, and it's very good. Try substituting leeks for the endives on occasion. The gingerbread recipe comes from our cook, Margaret Feely. She says it's Irish gingerbread, and I say it's great.

ENDIVES IN HAM, CHEESE SAUCE

(6–8 Servings)

8 medium-size endives
1 cup chicken stock
Juice of 1 lemon
Salt
8 slices boiled ham, trimmed of fat and thinly sliced
⅓ cup Swiss cheese, grated

Remove hearts from 8 medium-size endives, wash carefully and drain. Braise endives in large skillet in 1 cup chicken stock, juice of 1 lemon and pinch of salt. Bring liquid to a boil; cover skillet, lower heat and simmer for 2 minutes. (Endives should still be firm.) Drain. Wrap each endive in a thin slice of boiled ham.

SAUCE

2 cups milk, heated
3 tablespoons butter
2 tablespoons flour
1 teaspoon salt
½ teaspoon white pepper
¾ cup Swiss cheese, grated

Heat 2 cups milk in top of double boiler. Melt 3 tablespoons butter in saucepan; add 2 tablespoons flour, 1 teaspoon salt, ½ teaspoon white pepper, and cook for 3 minutes, stirring constantly with wooden spoon. Remove saucepan from heat and add hot milk gradually while stirring until sauce is smooth. Replace saucepan over heat and continue to stir until sauce has thickened. Add ¾ cup grated Swiss cheese and cook until cheese has melted. Pour some of sauce into baking dish; arrange 8 endives wrapped in ham in baking dish and cover with remaining sauce. Before serving, sprinkle ⅓ cup grated Swiss cheese over top, put under moderate broiler to heat and to brown top lightly.

GINGERBREAD

(8–10 Servings)

¼ pound butter, softened (1 bar)
1 cup sugar
2 eggs, beaten
Salt
3 cups flour, sifted
2 teaspoons ginger
1 teaspoon cinnamon
1 teaspoon cloves, ground
1 teaspoon baking soda
2 tablespoons boiling water
1 cup strong cold coffee
1 cup molasses

Preheat oven to 350°

Using a large bowl because mixture foams, cream ¼ pound butter and 1 cup sugar; add 2 eggs, well beaten, and pinch of salt.

Sift 3 cups flour with 2 teaspoons ginger, 1 teaspoon cinnamon, 1 teaspoon ground cloves and 1 teaspoon baking soda. Add these dry ingredients gradually to butter-sugar-egg mixture. Add 2 tablespoons boiling water, 1 cup strong cold coffee and 1 cup molasses. Blend thoroughly and pour into 2 greased pans 8 x 8-inches. Bake at 350° for 45 minutes.

MENU 7

Jellied Chicken Consommé
Baked Snapper with Crabmeat, Mousseline Sauce*
Italian Bread Mixed Vegetable Salad Chablis
Raspberry-Cheese Pie*

The Raspberry-Cheese Pie is marvelous but very rich; so I've kept the rest of the meal rather light. The mixed vegetable salad can include cooked or raw vegetables—or a combination of both.

BAKED SNAPPER WITH CRABMEAT

(*8 Servings*)

2 4-pound red snappers, cleaned and fileted (4 pieces)
1 pound lump crabmeat
Salt
Pepper
3 teaspoons dried dill weed (or 3 tablespoons fresh chopped dill)
3 tablespoons lemon juice
12 tablespoons butter, melted (1½ bars)

Preheat oven to 425°

Place 2 fileted pieces of 2 4-pound red snappers in shallow oiled baking dish. Pick over 1 pound lump crabmeat to remove cartilege and toss it gently with salt and pepper to taste, 3 teaspoons dried dill weed (or 3 tablespoons fresh chopped dill), 3 tablespoons lemon juice and 6 tablespoons melted butter. Spread ½ crabmeat mixture over pieces of snapper already in dish and cover with 2 remaining pieces. Secure with skewers. Pour remaining melted butter (6 tablespoons) over fish and bake for about 35–40 minutes in preheated 425° oven or until fish flakes easily. Arrange on warm serving platter. Remove skewers and garnish platter with crisp watercress or parsley as desired. Serve with Mousseline Sauce.

MOUSSELINE SAUCE

(6–8 Servings)

4 egg yolks
2 tablespoons lemon juice
½ pound butter, melted (2 bars)
Salt
Pepper
½ cup heavy cream, whipped

Put 4 egg yolks in blender; add 2 tablespoons lemon juice and blend quickly. Set blender to slow speed and gradually add ½ pound melted butter. Blend for 2–3 minutes or until sauce thickens. Salt and pepper to taste. Whip ½ cup heavy cream until stiff and fold into sauce.

RASPBERRY-CHEESE PIE

(8–10 Servings)

CRUST

1 small box graham crackers (6¾ ounces)
⅔ cup sugar
¼ pound butter, softened (1 bar)

Roll graham crackers fine. Blend together with ⅔ cup sugar and ¼ pound softened butter. Press mixture firmly and evenly against sides and bottom of 9-inch pie plate. Refrigerate for at least 1 hour.

FILLING

¾ pound cream cheese (1½ 8-ounce packages)
2 eggs
½ cup sugar
½ teaspoon vanilla extract
Cinnamon
2 cups raspberries, thawed (2 10-ounce packages frozen)
1 pint sour cream
3 tablespoons sugar
1 teaspoon vanilla extract

Preheat oven to 375°

Mix together in blender: ¾ pound cream cheese, 2 eggs, ½ cup sugar, ½ teaspoon vanilla extract and a dash of cinnamon. Drain juice from 2 cups raspberries, and fold raspberries gently into cream-cheese mixture. (Juice may be strained and frozen and reserved for future use as a sauce.) Pour into 9-inch pie plate that has been prepared as above. Bake in 375° oven for 20–25 minutes. Cool pie.

Blend 1 pint sour cream with 3 tablespoons sugar and 1 teaspoon vanilla extract and cover pie with cream. Return to oven for 5 minutes. (This pie may be made a day in advance and refrigerated, or it can be frozen. Strawberries or blueberries may be substituted for raspberries.)

MENU 8

	Jellied Beef Consommé	
Italian Brown Bread	Pasta Maison*	White Chianti
	Artichokes Vinaigrette	
	Pineapple Sherbet	

Just writing down the recipe for this pasta makes me hungry! Pineapple sherbet is especially inviting when it's served with green Crème de Menthe.

PASTA MAISON

(8–10 Servings)

¼ pound butter (1 bar)
1 pound mushrooms, sliced
Salt
Pepper
⅛ teaspoon marjoram
½ cup dry vermouth
2 cups frozen peas
1 pound boiled ham, trimmed of fat and cubed
4 white truffles, sliced (optional)

¼ pound butter (1 bar)
1 pound pasta (farfalle or capelletti or elbow macaroni)
6 quarts boiling water
2 tablespoons salt
2 tablespoons oil
1 cup freshly grated Parmesan cheese
1 cup lightly whipped cream
Freshly ground black pepper

Melt ¼ pound butter in skillet, add 1 pound mushrooms, sliced, ⅛ teaspoon marjoram, salt and pepper to taste. Cover and cook for about 10 minutes, stirring occasionally. Add ½ cup dry vermouth, 2 cups frozen peas, 1 pound boiled ham, trimmed of fat and cubed, and, if available, 4 white truffles, sliced. Cook another 10 minutes; remove from heat and reserve. Melt a second ¼ pound butter and set aside. Put 1 pound pasta in 6 quarts boiling water to which 2 tablespoons salt and 2 tablespoons oil have been added. When water returns to the boil, start timing and boil for 12 minutes. Pour pasta into colander in sink, drain, and pour boiling water over pasta. Put melted butter in heated serving dish, add pasta and ½ cup freshly grated Parmesan cheese. Add mushrooms, peas, ham and truffles and 1 cup lightly whipped cream. Toss gently until well mixed. Sprinkle with freshly ground black pepper, remaining ½ cup Parmesan cheese and serve.

MENU 9

Mackerel in White Wine
French Bread   Poached Chicken, Sauce Maison*   Pouilly Fuissé

Rice Ring Filled with Peas
Chocolate Roll with Ice Cream

The mackerel in white wine comes from abroad in long, flat tins. They are murder to open but well worth the effort. Prepare the chocolate roll in advance, using any good recipe and filling the roll with softened vanilla ice cream. Wrap the roll in aluminum foil and freeze it.

POACHED CHICKEN, SAUCE MAISON

(8–10 Servings)

2 3–3½-pound fryers
1 lemon, cut in half
4 carrots, scraped and cut up
4 onions, cut up
8 stalks celery and their tops
8 sprigs parsley
4 small bay leaves
2 tablespoons salt
½ cup fresh tarragon leaves (or ⅛ cup dried)
1 cup dry white wine
½ cup heavy cream
6 egg yolks

Rinse chickens well under cold water. Pat dry. Rub each chicken with ½ lemon. Put chickens in large kettle with cold water barely to cover. Bring liquid to a boil and skim well. Add 4 carrots, scraped and cut up, 4 onions, cut up, 8 stalks celery and their tops, 8 sprigs parsley, 4 small bay leaves, 2 tablespoons salt and ½ cup fresh tarragon leaves. Reduce heat and let broth simmer very slowly for about 35 minutes or until juice in chicken legs runs clear when legs are pierced with a fork. Remove chickens and keep them warm. Cook broth briskly over high heat for about 45 minutes to reduce liquid and strengthen it. Strain broth and pour into top of large double boiler. Add 1 cup dry white wine and cook 2 or 3 minutes. Blend ½ cup heavy cream with 6 egg yolks. Pour a little hot broth over cream and eggs, then return all together. Correct seasoning and keep sauce warm but do not boil. On carving board, remove skin from chicken and pull meat from bones in large pieces. Arrange pieces of chicken on heated serving platter and pour a little sauce over all. Serve remaining sauce separately. (If any sauce is left, it can be frozen to reappear in any number of dishes.)

MENU 10

Senegalese Soup
Gnocchi alla Romana, Tomato Sauce*
Italian Bread | Mixed Green Salad | Riesling
Lichee Nuts
Macaroons

Senegalese is a lovely curried soup made with a base of chicken stock. The gnocchi in the recipe (which are really small dumplings) are made with semolina, and they are lighter than those made of flour. Fresh lichee nuts are available only in June and July, but the canned variety is delicious, too. I often use them in a mixed compote or in a trifle, where their unusual flavor makes a real contribution to the dish.

GNOCCHI ALLA ROMANA, TOMATO SAUCE

(8–10 Servings)

4 small onions, peeled
2 bay leaves
2 quarts milk
2½ cups semolina
1 teaspoon salt
4 egg yolks
1 cup freshly grated Parmesan cheese
¼ pound butter (1 bar)
4 teaspoons Dijon mustard
¼ pound butter, melted (1 bar)
Additional grated Parmesan cheese
Salt
Pepper

Preheat oven to 400°

Put 4 peeled onions and 2 bay leaves in 2 quarts milk and bring slowly to a boil. Remove and discard onions and bay leaves. Sift 2½ cups semolina with 1 teaspoon salt into hot milk, stirring constantly. Simmer 5–10 minutes, or until mixture has thickened. Remove from heat and stir in 4 egg yolks, 1 cup freshly grated Parmesan cheese, ¼ pound butter and 4 teaspoons Dijon mustard. Blend well and spread mixture evenly (¾-inch thick) on a cookie sheet that has been moistened with cold water. Refrigerate. When quite cold, cut into 2-inch rounds with biscuit cutter (or small glass). Arrange in oven-proof serving dish and sprinkle with ¼ pound melted butter and additional grated Parmesan cheese. Bake in preheated 400° oven for 15 minutes. Put under hot broiler just before serving and season to taste with salt and freshly ground pepper. Gnocchi may be served without sauce, but the tomato sauce in the following recipe goes well with gnocchi and other pastas.

TOMATO SAUCE

(8–10 Servings)

¼ pound butter (1 bar)
4 onions, chopped
4 pounds tomatoes (about 14 medium-size), peeled and quartered
6 sprigs parsley
6 sprigs thyme
4 cloves
Grated nutmeg
4 shallots, peeled and chopped
1 can tomato paste
1 cup chicken stock

Melt ¼ pound butter and sauté 4 chopped onions until they are translucent. Add 4 pounds peeled and quartered tomatoes and stir over high heat for 5 minutes. Add 6 sprigs parsley, 6 sprigs thyme, 4 cloves, some grated nutmeg, 4 chopped shallots, 1 can tomato paste and 1 cup chicken stock. Cover pot and simmer for 1 hour. Strain, correct seasoning and serve with gnocchi. (Sauce may be frozen and served with other pasta in the future.)

MENU 11

Onion Soup
Hard Rolls — Bay Scallops — Chablis
Potatoes Boiled in Jackets
Vegetable Purée
Bread-and-Butter Pudding*

I suggest omitting the conventional slices of bread in the onion soup if you plan to follow this menu and serve Bread-and-Butter Pudding, a favorite among gourmets because it is so simple that it is truly sophisticated.

BREAD-AND-BUTTER PUDDING

(6–8 Servings)

8 thin slices white bread, crusts removed
Butter
⅔ cup golden seedless raisins
4 eggs
¼ cup sugar
1 quart milk
Grated nutmeg

Preheat oven to 350°

Grease a deep glass pie plate or 10-inch casserole dish. Remove crusts and butter bread on one side. Cut bread into triangles or squares and lay neatly in pie plate buttered-side-up. Sprinkle ⅔ cup raisins over bread. Beat 4 eggs with ¼ cup sugar; add 1 quart milk and stir until smooth. Pour mixture over bread and let stand for 30 minutes. Bake at 350° until custard is set (approximately 45 minutes to 1 hour). Sprinkle with grated nutmeg or ground cinnamon. May be served with cream if desired.

MENU 12

Home-Style Chicken Soup*
Italian Bread   Cheese-and-Wine Casserole*   Sangría
Field Salad
Rhubarb-and-Strawberry Compote
Cookies

The Casserole is heartier than a cheese soufflé but much less rich than a quiche. It takes almost no time to make, and it's foolproof. Sangría is served very often in Spain during warm weather. It is usually made with red wine, lemon juice, soda or water, sugar, berries or other fresh fruit in season.

HOME-STYLE CHICKEN SOUP

(2–2½ quarts)

2 fowl
2 teaspoons salt
1 teaspoon black peppercorns
4 carrots, scraped and cut up
1 bunch leeks, trimmed
1 bunch celery and their tops
6 sprigs parsley

Wash 2 fowl and pat dry; place fowl in large kettle with cold water to cover. Add 2 teaspoons salt, 1 teaspoon black peppercorns, 4 carrots, cut up, 1 bunch trimmed leeks, 1 bunch celery with tops and 6 sprigs parsley. Bring to a boil. Cover pot, lower heat and simmer slowly for 4 hours. Strain soup and allow to cool. Reserve vegetables. Remove chicken breasts (which can be used at another time); replace rest of chickens in same pot with vegetables; add 1 quart boiling water and allow to simmer for 1 more hour. Strain and add to first batch. Correct seasoning. When soup is cool, remove fat from surface. Store in freezer if desired.

CHEESE-AND-WINE CASSEROLE

(8–10 Servings)

12 tablespoons butter (1½ bars)
6 shallots, chopped and crushed
12 slices white bread, trimmed
12 eggs
1 cup heavy cream
3 cups dry white wine
1 cup chicken stock
1 pound Gruyère cheese, grated
½ teaspoon dry mustard
2 teaspoons paprika

Preheat oven to 350°

Cream 12 tablespoons butter with 6 chopped and crushed shallots and spread evenly on 12 slices trimmed white bread. Arrange bread in two 1½-quart heat-proof dishes (6 slices in each dish) buttered-side-down. Beat 12 eggs until foamy; beat in 1 cup heavy cream. Add 3 cups dry white wine, 1 cup chicken stock, 1 pound grated Gruyère cheese, ½ teaspoon dry mustard, 2 teaspoons paprika, and blend well. Pour ½ total amount over bread in each dish and bake in preheated 350° oven for 30 minutes or until puffed and brown.

MENU 13

Crème Olga*
Boeuf à la Mode with Aspic Trick
Toasted Rye Bread Tabbooli* Beer
String Bean Salad
Strawberry Soufflé*

The "aspic trick" is something I learned by watching Rudolf Stanish. To save time, pour your aspic onto a shallow four-sided cookie sheet that is approximately the same size as your meat platter. Chill the aspic; arrange the sliced beef on a cold platter and when the aspic is set, turn the cookie sheet upside down over the meat platter, tapping it so that the aspic covers the beef. Chop the excess aspic and arrange it around the sides of the platter. (This isn't as beautiful as the more orthodox method of coating the meat slices layer by layer, but it is lots easier and much faster.) The Strawberry Soufflé is incredibly light, fragrant and delicious. It's also low in calories.

CRÈME OLGA

(6–8 Servings)

8 bunches scallions
1 cup water
2 teaspoons salt
1 teaspoon white pepper
8 cups chicken stock
½ cup rice flour
2 cups light cream

¼ pound raw mushrooms, chopped
2 tablespoons chives, chopped

Trim and cut up 8 bunches scallions and cook slowly in a deep pan with 1 cup water, 2 teaspoons salt and 1 teaspoon white pepper until mushy. Add 1 cup chicken stock to ½ cup rice flour and stir until smooth. Add this and rest of chicken stock (7 cups) to pan and bring to a boil. Simmer for 15 minutes; let cool. Pour liquid into blender and blend until smooth.* Add 2 cups light cream and pour into cups. Chill. Sprinkle chopped raw mushrooms and chopped chives on top. (Raw chopped cucumbers and minced dill make a delicious alternate garnish.)

* When desired, freeze soup at this point.

TABBOOLI

(6–8 Servings)

2 cups cracked wheat
1 cup parsley, finely chopped
½ cup onions, finely chopped
2 tomatoes, peeled, seeds removed and chopped
1 cup lemon juice
1 cup salad oil
Salt
Pepper
2 tomatoes, peeled and quartered with seeds removed

Cover 2 cups cracked wheat with boiling water and let stand for 2 hours. (If water is absorbed after 1 hour, cover with more water and continue soaking for the remaining hour.) Drain and squeeze excess water from wheat. Toss wheat lightly in a large bowl with 1 cup finely chopped parsley, ½ cup finely chopped onions, 2 chopped tomatoes, 1 cup lemon juice, 1 cup salad oil and salt and pepper to taste. Garnish with 2 tomatoes, peeled, quartered and seeded.

STRAWBERRY SOUFFLÉ

(4–6 Servings)

1 cup strawberry pulp (contents of 1 10-ounce package frozen strawberries)
5 egg whites, stiffly beaten
Salt
6 tablespoons confectioner's sugar
Strawberry juice
Sugar
Kirsch

Preheat oven to 350°

Thaw 1 10-ounce package frozen strawberries, drain and reserve juice. Beat 5 egg whites with a pinch of salt until foamy; add 6 tablespoons confectioner's sugar gradually, and continue beating until whites stand in peaks. Gently fold in 1 cup strawberry pulp and pile mixture into lightly buttered 1-quart soufflé dish so that center is higher than sides. Bake for 30 minutes in preheated 350° oven. Sugar reserved strawberry juice to taste and add about 2 teaspoons Kirsch. Serve sauce separately with soufflé.

MENU 14

Artichoke Bottoms with Mushrooms and French Dressing
Croissants Risotto with Chicken Livers* Tavel

Mixed Green Salad
Chocolate Bavarian Cream

This first course can be part of your stock-on-hand canned foods, and it's especially useful for unexpected guests. I like to use chanterelles (those marvelous wild French mushrooms), but the little button mushrooms in brine or even raw sliced ones will do nicely.

RISOTTO WITH CHICKEN LIVERS

(6–8 Servings)

1 pound chicken livers (fresh and young)
2 tablespoons oil
2 tablespoons onions, chopped
6 large mushrooms, sliced
2 teaspoons tomato paste
2 cups rice
5 cups strong chicken stock (4 10-ounce cans)
6 tablespoons Parmesan cheese (freshly grated)
3 tablespoons butter, cut into 6 pieces

Using a deep skillet, sauté 1 pound chicken livers in 2 tablespoons hot oil until livers are just brown. Remove livers and keep them warm. Add 2 tablespoons chopped onions to pan. Cook until onions are translucent. Add 6 large sliced mushrooms; and, after 2 minutes, stir in 2 teaspoons tomato paste. Add 2 cups rice and cook over low heat for 5 minutes. Cover rice with 5 cups strong chicken stock and continue cooking slowly until rice has absorbed stock and is "al dente." When rice is nearly done, replace livers. Transfer risotto to heated serving dish and sprinkle grated Parmesan cheese over top. Dot with 6 pieces of butter (3 tablespoons) and allow butter to permeate rice.

MENU 15

Leeks Vinaigrette
Italian Bread — Meat Loaf* — Beer
Rice and Onions
Snow Peas
Chocolate Torte, Custard Sauce*

Leeks vinaigrette can take the place of a salad in other menus. (Use only the white parts of the leeks.) The Meat Loaf is good both hot and cold; so be sure to make an extra one to serve cold. To make the rice and onions, sauté the onions in hot oil; add the rice, cooking until each grain is coated with oil. Cover the rice with twice as much liquid as rice, and cook slowly until the liquid is absorbed and the rice is done.

MEAT LOAF

(6–8 Servings)

1 pound beef, ground
½ pound veal, ground
½ pound pork, ground
1 cup bread crumbs
½ cup tomato juice
½ teaspoon salt
⅛ teaspoon pepper

2 eggs, slightly beaten
1 medium onion, chopped fine
2 teaspoons mixed herbs (chives, tarragon, chervil, fennel)
1½ tablespoons Worcestershire Sauce
½ teaspoon monosodium glutamate
1 tablespoon butter, softened
2 tablespoons parsley, chopped
3 hard-cooked eggs, shelled
½ cup beef stock

Preheat oven to 400°

In large bowl, mix together all ingredients except softened butter, chopped parsley, hard-cooked eggs and beef stock. Grease loaf pan and fill with ½ of mixture. Place 3 hard-cooked and shelled eggs lengthwise in center of mixture and cover with remaining half of meat mixture. Spread 1 tablespoon softened butter over top of loaf. Bake in preheated 400° oven for 1½ hours, basting every 20 minutes. (Use beef stock if necessary.) When done, remove to heated platter. Sprinkle chopped parsley over top of loaf. Slice and serve with brown sauce.

SAUCE

2 tablespoons cornstarch
1½ cups beef stock
Maggi
Salt
Pepper

Dissolve 2 tablespoons cornstarch in ½ cup beef stock. Pour off fat from drippings in loaf pan. Place pan over heat and add dissolved cornstarch to the drippings; add dash of Maggi and 1 cup beef stock. Season to taste. Simmer, stirring constantly, until sauce is slightly thickened. Strain sauce and serve with meat loaf.

CHOCOLATE TORTE

(8–10 Servings)

2½ squares bitter chocolate
1 tablespoon brandy (or rum)
1 tablespoon water
¼ pound butter (1 bar)
½ cup sugar
5 egg yolks
1 egg
1 cup almonds, ground
5 egg whites, beaten stiff

Preheat oven to 350°

Melt 2½ squares bitter chocolate with 1 tablespoon brandy and 1 tablespoon water. Cream ¼ pound butter with ½ cup sugar; add 5 egg yolks and 1 whole egg and blend thoroughly. Add 1 cup ground almonds and cooled, melted chocolate. Beat 5 egg whites until stiff and fold gently into mixture. Pour into lightly buttered springform pan (7–8 inches in diameter. Bake at 350° for 45 minutes to 1 hour. Serve with the following custard sauce:

CUSTARD SAUCE

2 egg yolks
¼ cup sugar
¼ teaspoon salt

1½ cups light cream
1 tablespoon Kirsch or brandy

With wire whisk, beat 2 egg yolks lightly in top of double boiler. Blend in ¼ cup sugar; add ¼ teaspoon salt and 1½ cups light cream. Cook over simmering (not boiling) water, stirring constantly. When custard thinly coats metal spoon, remove from heat. Add 1 tablespoon Kirsch or brandy. Chill.

MENU 16

Watercress Soup
Poached Bass in Aspic with Truffles, Shrimp and Tomatoes*
French Bread   Cheese Salad*   Chilean Riesling
Oranges in Red Wine

The Poached Bass can be a beautiful picture with the contrast of the truffles, tomatoes and shrimp under the shiny aspic. Do take it out of the refrigerator once the aspic is set and keep it just cool enough to prevent the aspic from melting. The Cheese Salad is unusually good, but as it's quite rich, I've chosen a simple dessert.

POACHED BASS IN ASPIC WITH TRUFFLES, SHRIMP AND TOMATOES

(6–8 Servings)

COURT-BOUILLON

1 quart dry white wine
1 quart clam juice

1 quart cold water
2 medium onions, peeled and sliced
2 medium carrots, peeled and cut up
8 whole black peppercorns, slightly bruised
1 tablespoon salt
4 stalks celery and their tops
6 sprigs parsley
2 whole bay leaves
1 pound bones of white-meat fish (if available)
4–5-pound striped bass, cleaned but with head and tail left on
1 pound cooked shrimp
3–4 large tomatoes, skinned, seeded and quartered
2 truffles, finely chopped

Put 1 quart dry white wine, 1 quart clam juice, 1 quart water, 2 medium onions, sliced, 2 medium carrots, cut up, 8 slightly bruised whole peppercorns, 1 tablespoon salt, 4 stalks celery and their tops, 6 sprigs parsley and 2 whole bay leaves into an enamel fish poacher. If available, add 1 pound bones of white-meat fish. Bring to a boil; turn down heat and barely simmer bouillon for 30 minutes. Strain. Place 4–5-pound cleaned striped bass (but with head and tail left on) in poacher and cover with court-bouillon. Bring slowly to a boil. Place poacher over 2 burners on flame tamers and turn heat down very low. Poach fish gently for about 40–45 minutes or until fish flakes easily. Remove from heat and allow fish to cool in bouillon. While fish is cooling, make following aspic:

ASPIC

1 envelope gelatin
1 cup cold court-bouillon (strained through 3 layers of cheesecloth wrung out of cold water)

1 cup boiling court-bouillon (strained through 3 layers of cheesecloth wrung out of cold water)
1½ teaspoons brandy

Soften 1 envelope gelatin in 1 cup strained cold court-bouillon; and 1 cup strained boiling court-bouillon and stir over heat until gelatin has dissolved. Refrigerate.

Lift fish onto cold serving platter (draining over poacher for a moment). Leave skin on head and tail, but remove skin from top half of body of fish carefully. Remove bones gently. (Cover eye of fish with slice of truffle, or carrot, or other vegetable.) When aspic has become syrupy, brush fish with first coat of aspic. (Keep remaining aspic syrupy.) Arrange 1 pound cooked shrimp and tomato quarters around platter and brush them with aspic, too. Chill in refrigerator. When aspic on platter has set, brush fish, shrimp and tomatoes again with syrupy aspic and sprinkle finely chopped truffles over all. Chill again. Refrigerate remaining aspic and when it is firm, chop up and put around platter. Garnish with crisp parsley or watercress. Serve with mayonnaise to which a generous amount of chopped fresh dill has been added. (If fresh dill is not available, use ¼ the amount of dried dill weed.)

CHEESE SALAD

(8–10 Servings)

12 hard-cooked eggs
1 pound Bel Paese (or other mild, firm cheese)
2 cups sour cream
1 cup mayonnaise
2 tablespoons caraway seeds
2 tablespoons horseradish

Salt
Pepper

Chop hard-cooked eggs; cut cheese in strips. In a bowl, blend 2 cups sour cream, 1 cup mayonnaise, 2 tablespoons caraway seeds and 2 tablespoons horseradish. Season to taste with salt and pepper. Add eggs and cheese to dressing. Chill and serve.

MENU 17

Icelandic Trout, Yogurt-and-Red-Caviar Sauce
Roast Filet of Beef*
Croissants — Parsleyed Potato Balls — Red Burgundy
Field Salad
Macedoine of Fruit with Kirsch
Madeleines

The Icelandic trout comes in tins. It is a small pink-fleshed fish with a delicate flavor. Red caviar mixed with plain yogurt makes a good sauce to serve with it. If yogurt isn't among your favorites, try pink mayonnaise made by adding ⅓ cup tomato paste, the juice of 1 lemon, a teaspoon of grated lemon rind and some seasoning to 1 cup of mayonnaise. When guests are late, the Filet of Beef can be kept pink and juicy by wrapping it in aluminum foil and keeping it in a warm place—not the oven.

ROAST FILET OF BEEF

(6–8 Servings)

1 whole filet of beef, wrapped with suet
Monosodium glutamate
Salt
Pepper
1 truffle, finely chopped (optional)

Preheat oven to 500°

Sprinkle dash of monosodium glutamate on beef and place it in an uncovered roasting pan in preheated 500° oven for 15 minutes. Baste at least once. Lower oven temperature to 400° and continue to roast for another 15 minutes, basting at least once. Sprinkle with salt and pepper. Reduce heat again to 350° for last 15 minutes and baste during this interval too. Remove filet from oven.

SAUCE

2 tablespoons cornstarch
4 tablespoons cold beef stock
1¼ cups hot beef stock
Salt
Pepper
Bovril
3 tablespoons fresh tarragon, coarsely chopped (optional)

Dissolve 2 tablespoons cornstarch in 4 tablespoons cold beef stock. Pour off fat from drippings in roasting pan and discard. Put roasting pan on top of range; add 1¼ cups hot beef stock to drippings and scrape brown bits from sides of pan to enrich sauce. Add cornstarch mixture, stirring constantly, until sauce is smooth and slightly thickened. Season to taste with salt, pepper and a few drops of Bovril (or Maggi or Kitchen Bouquet). Strain sauce into top half of double boiler and add 3 tablespoons coarsely chopped tarragon (optional). Re-heat sauce at time of serving. Meanwhile, put filet on carving board and remove foil; cut strings and lift off suet. Correct seasoning. Carve filet in ½-inch slices and arrange on heated serving platter. (It should still be medium rare.) Add beef juices to sauce and stir until it is blended. Sprinkle 1 finely chopped truffle over top of filet (optional). Arrange bouquets of vegetables and parsleyed potato balls around beef. (I often use slices of pâté around platter and artichoke bottoms topped with purée of carrots.) Serve sauce separately.

MENU 18

Cold Borscht

Italian Bread — Lobster Salad Maison* — Chablis

Raw Baby Zucchini, French Dressing

Strawberry Shortcake

I add some chopped hard-cooked eggs and a dash of sour cream to the borscht. The baby zucchini are so tender that I don't peel them before slicing them into ¼-inch rounds.

LOBSTER SALAD MAISON

(6–8 Servings)

2 pounds cooked lobster meat, cut into bite-size pieces
1 pound fresh mushrooms, stems removed
2 cans small artichoke hearts (approximately 20–24 hearts)
1 cup mayonnaise
½ cup fresh dill, finely chopped (or 2 tablespoons dried dill weed)
Salt
White pepper

In a large bowl, mix 2 pounds cooked lobster with 1 pound mushrooms (if mushrooms are large, cut them in half or in quarters), contents of 2 cans small artichoke hearts, 1 cup mayonnaise and ½ cup finely chopped fresh dill. Season to taste with salt and white pepper. Place in salad bowl; chill and serve.

MENU 19

Asparagus, Hollandaise Sauce (or Vinaigrette)
Rye Bread — Hungarian Beef Stew* — Red Bordeaux
Fettucini
Spinach-and-Bacon Salad
Apricot Tart*

The asparagus can be fresh or those lovely thick white canned ones. Whether to use Vinaigrette or Hollandaise might depend on the weather or your preference. The fettucini should be cooked "al dente," drained and tossed with cream, butter, freshly grated Parmesan cheese and sprinkled with freshly ground black pepper.

HUNGARIAN BEEF STEW

(6–8 Servings)

5 medium onions, chopped
4 tablespoons butter
2 pounds chuck, fat removed, and meat cut in 1½-inch squares
½ teaspoon salt
Marjoram
¼ teaspoon pepper
3 shallots, finely chopped
¾ cup dry white wine
¼ pound sliced bacon
2 cups sour cream

Brown 5 chopped onions in 4 tablespoons butter. Add 2 pounds chuck, ½ teaspoon salt, dash of marjoram, ¼ teaspoon pepper and 3 finely chopped shallots. Stir in ¾ cup dry white wine; cover and simmer slowly for approximately 45 minutes or until the meat is nearly tender. Brown ¼ pound bacon in a separate frying pan; drain on paper toweling; break into pieces and add to meat. (If you plan to freeze the stew, do so at this point. Before serving, thaw completely and follow remaining directions.) Stir in 2 cups sour cream, cover and continue cooking for ½ hour or until meat is tender.

APRICOT TART

(8–10 Servings)

½ pound dried apricots
½ cup sugar
1 baked 9-inch tart shell (recipe page 173)
Custard sauce (recipe page 195–196, but double number of egg yolks)
¾ cup apricot jam
2 tablespoons water

Cover ½ pound dried apricots with hot water and allow to soak at least 2 hours or, if possible, overnight. Cover fruit with water, add ½ cup sugar and simmer over low heat for 8–10 minutes. Drain and cool. Spread custard thinly over bottom of tart shell and arrange apricot halves (skin side up) in overlapping circles, using as much fruit as possible. Melt ¾ cup apricot jam with 2 tablespoons water in top half of double boiler. Strain and glaze apricots.

Fresh blue plums (cut in half lengthwise and pitted) may be substituted for apricots when they are in season. Proceed as for apricot tart, but use apple jelly to make fruit glaze.

MENU 20

Quiche
Mixed Seafood in Special Sauce*
French Bread — Cucumber Sandwiches — Soave
Rice
Raw Mushroom Salad
Pears in Red Wine
Cookies

A quiche has many variations, and there are some excellent ones to be bought either frozen or freshly made for you to freeze. If you have an unsweetened pastry shell in your freezer, you can invent your own. Try mixing some sliced onions with the basic custard-and-cheese mixture. The cucumber sandwiches should be very small. Use thinly sliced white bread with the crusts removed, and be sure the sliced cucumbers have been crisped in salted ice water, then pressed dry before being put on the bread.

SPECIAL SAUCE FOR SEAFOOD DISH

(6–8 Servings)

4 tablespoons butter
10 shallots, finely chopped
2 tablespoons English mustard
1 cup medium cream
1 cup dry white wine
1 lump sugar
Salt
Paprika

Melt 4 tablespoons butter in deep skillet, and sauté 10 finely chopped shallots until softened. Blend 2 tablespoons English mustard in ¼ cup medium cream, and add to pan. Add 1 cup dry white wine, 1 lump sugar, salt to taste and balance of cream (¾ cup). Use enough paprika to color sauce faintly pink. Simmer over low heat for 10 minutes while heating seafood in sauce.

SUGGESTED COMBINATIONS OF SEAFOOD

1 pound cooked lobster meat
1 pound cooked small shrimp
2 cans mussels and their liquid

or

1 pound cooked lobster meat
1 pound cooked bay scallops
2 cans minced clams and their liquid

MENU 21

Cold Lemon Soup*
Italian Bread — Veal Scallops Rossini* — Pouilly Fumé
Baby Lima Beans
Mixed Green Salad
Trifle

The Lemon Soup is modeled after the recipe for Greek Lemon Soup I gave in *My Favorite Things*, except that I have now learned how delicate it becomes when it is served very cold on a hot summer day. I find, however, that the amount of rice should be cut to ¼ cup. Trifle is one of those dishes that can be varied endlessly according to what you have on hand.

COLD LEMON SOUP

(*8 Servings*)

3 quarts clear chicken broth
¼ cup rice

4 egg whites
4 egg yolks
½ cup strained lemon juice
Salt
Pepper

Bring 3 quarts clear chicken broth to boiling point. Wash ¼ cup rice, add to broth and cook until soft, or for about 20 minutes. When rice is cooked, turn off heat. In a large mixing bowl beat 4 egg whites until stiff, then add 4 yolks and continue beating, adding gradually ½ cup strained lemon juice. Add the broth and rice, a little at a time, beating constantly with large whisk. Pour this mixture back into pot. Place on low heat and bring barely to boiling point, stirring constantly. Remove from heat; allow to cool. Season to taste with salt and pepper and serve well chilled.

VEAL SCALLOPS ROSSINI

(6–8 Servings)

1½ ounces dried mushrooms
3 pounds veal scallops, thinly sliced (12 scallops)
12 tablespoons butter, melted (1½ bars)
2 medium truffles, finely chopped
½ cup Madeira wine
2 tablespoons cornstarch
¼ cup beef stock
Salt
Pepper
12 slices pâté

Cover 1½ ounces dried mushrooms with water and let stand for

15–20 minutes or until soft and plump. Pound 12 veal scallops between 2 pieces waxed paper to ¼-inch thickness. Dust scallops with seasoned flour and sauté quickly in 8 tablespoons melted butter until golden brown. Remove from pan and keep warm on heated platter. Put remaining 4 tablespoons melted butter in same pan, add 2 finely chopped truffles and ½ cup Madeira wine and cook for 2–3 minutes. Dissolve 2 tablespoons cornstarch in ¼ cup beef stock and add to sauce, stirring well. Drain mushrooms, add to sauce and cook long enough to heat through. Season to taste with salt and pepper. Pour sauce over veal slices and arrange slices of pâté around platter.

MENU 22

Vichyssoise with Minced Clams
French Bread — Lime-Broiled Chicken* — Iced Tea
Zucchini and Tomatoes*
Rice Pilaf
Brown Betty

There are some excellent canned Vichyssoises on the market, and I have found that by adding canned minced clams and their juice to the Vichyssoise, you can serve a very good mock clam chowder—either hot or cold. The Lime-Broiled Chicken has a most unusual flavor. It is also very good served cold. The Zucchini and Tomatoes provide the color to make this meal attractive to look at, and Brown Betty, an old favorite of mine, is as easy to make as to eat.

LIME-BROILED CHICKEN

(6–8 Servings)

4 whole chicken breasts (8 halves, boned and skin removed)
2¼ teaspoons salt
Monosodium glutamate
1¼ cups corn oil
1¼ cups lime juice
5 tablespoons onion, chopped
5 teaspoons dried tarragon (or 5 tablespoons fresh)
1¼ teaspoons Tabasco

Sprinkle 8 half chicken breasts with 2¼ teaspoons salt; add dash monosodium glutamate and marinate chicken in 1¼ cups corn oil, 1¼ cups lime juice, 5 tablespoons chopped onion, 5 teaspoons dried tarragon (or 5 tablespoons fresh) and 1¼ teaspoons Tabasco for at least 4 hours. Broil breasts in deep baking dish in marinade under moderate heat for 2–3 minutes on each side. If fresh tarragon is available, sprinkle some on breasts. Transfer breasts to heated serving platter (discarding marinade) and serve with rice pilaf.

ZUCCHINI AND TOMATOES

(8–10 Servings)

4 large zucchini, sliced 1-inch thick
2 tablespoons butter
3 tablespoons water
½ teaspoon salt
¼ teaspoon freshly ground black pepper
2 tablespoons oil

1 tablespoon onion, chopped
3 large tomatoes, skinned and thinly sliced
⅓ cup freshly grated Parmesan cheese

Put 4 large sliced zucchini into saucepan and cover with water. Bring to a boil, drain and return zucchini to pan with 2 tablespoons butter, 3 tablespoons water, ½ teaspoon salt and ¼ teaspoon freshly ground black pepper. Cover saucepan and cook slowly until zucchini are just soft (about 20 minutes). Heat 2 tablespoons oil in skillet, add 1 tablespoon chopped onion and cook briskly for 2 minutes. Add tomatoes, sliced, and sauté them briefly on each side, being careful to keep slices whole. Transfer to oven-proof dish, arranging tomato slices in center, zucchini surrounding them. Pour onions over all. Sprinkle with grated Parmesan cheese and brown under moderate broiler just before serving.

MENU 23

Pâté Maison in Aspic*
French Bread　　Roast Chicken Tarragon*　　Alsatian Riesling
Rice Ring Filled with Carrots and Peas
Field Salad
Macedoine of Fruit with Sauterne
Marble Cake

I first tasted the pâté at my sister-in-law Wilhelmina's. It's particularly light and can be served either as a first course or with before-dinner drinks. The recipe for the roast chicken is as close as I can get to French roast chicken. Be sure to use fresh tarragon whenever possible. Try letting an ice cube melt into the French dressing for the field salad while you are beating the oil and vinegar. It thickens the dressing a bit and gives it a slightly different flavor.

PÂTÉ MAISON

(8–10 Servings)

½ pound raw fresh chicken livers
½ teaspoon salt
⅛ teaspoon white pepper
Cayenne
½ teaspoon marjoram
Nutmeg
1 small white onion, cut up
2 shallots, peeled and cut up
1 whole egg
1 egg yolk
1 egg white, beaten stiff
1 cup heavy cream, whipped

Preheat oven to 325°

Put ½ pound chicken livers, ½ teaspoon salt, ⅛ teaspoon white pepper, dash of cayenne, ½ teaspoon marjoram, dash of nutmeg, 1 small white onion, cut up, 2 shallots, peeled and cut up, 1 whole egg and 1 egg yolk in blender and blend until smooth. Beat 1 egg white until stiff but not dry. Beat 1 cup heavy cream until stiff. Fold egg white into cream and add this mixture to liver. Pour all into greased mold ⅔ full. Place mold in a shallow pan. Fill pan with 1½ inches water and bake at 325° for 1 hour.

ASPIC

1 tablespoon gelatin
1 tablespoon brandy
¾ cup beef stock

Soften 1 tablespoon gelatin in 1 tablespoon brandy; add ¼ cup beef stock and bring to a boil. Cool; when mixture is beginning to set, add the remaining ½ cup beef stock. When pâté has cooled, unmold on chilled serving dish and coat top and sides with aspic. Use rest of aspic, chopped, to surround mold. Garnish with truffles and parsley. Keep refrigerated until ready to serve.

ROAST CHICKEN TARRAGON

(6–8 Servings)

2 3½-pound fryers
8 tablespoons butter, softened (1 bar)
Salt
Monosodium glutamate
4 tablespoons fresh tarragon (or 1 tablespoon dried)
2 tablespoons cornstarch
2 cups strong chicken stock
2 tablespoons fresh tarragon, coarsely chopped (or 2 teaspoons dried)
Maggi

Preheat oven to 400°

Wipe chickens with damp towel and pat dry. Sprinkle cavities with salt and dash of monosodium glutamate. Put 2 tablespoons fresh tarragon (or ½ tablespoon dried) in cavity of each chicken, and spread each bird with 4 tablespoons softened butter. Place chickens in open roasting pan, breasts up, and roast for ½ hour in preheated 400° oven, basting every 15 minutes. Reduce heat to 350° and continue roasting and basting for 45 minutes more. Dissolve 2 tablespoons cornstarch in 1 cup chicken stock. When chickens are done, transfer them to carving board and keep them warm. Put roasting pan on top of range over low heat and add cornstarch to pan drippings. Stir a few minutes with wooden spoon and add balance of chicken stock (1 cup)—stirring constantly and incorporating brown bits from sides of pan. Add dash of Maggi and cook briskly for about 5 minutes to reduce liquid. Strain sauce, correct seasoning and add 2 tablespoons coarsely chopped tarragon leaves. Keep sauce hot in double boiler. Carve and arrange chickens on heated serving platter and serve with sauce passed separately.

MENU 24

Smoked Salmon

Italian Bread — Veal Marengo* — Pouilly Fuissé

Elbow Macaroni

Mixed Green Salad

Cold Lemon Soufflé*

I like to serve lemon wedges, capers and pumpernickel with the salmon. The Cold Soufflé is a fake, of course, as a soufflé, but it's wonderfully refreshing and light, and it can be prepared well ahead of time. In fact, the whole meal can be done in advance. Then, at serving time, reheat the elbow macaroni and toss with cream, butter, freshly ground black pepper and freshly grated Parmesan cheese.

VEAL MARENGO

(6–8 Servings)

4 pounds shoulder of veal cut into pieces about 2 inches square
1 cup onions, chopped fine
1 cup salad oil
½ cup flour
Salt
Pepper
1 cup dry white wine
½ cup tomato paste (or 4–5 very ripe plum tomatoes)
1 cup chicken stock
4 shallots, peeled
10 sprigs parsley, coarsely chopped
2 bay leaves
2 teaspoons crushed thyme leaves

Sauté 4 pounds veal and 1 cup finely chopped onions in 1 cup hot salad oil until lightly browned. Remove veal from frying pan and discard oil. Dust veal in seasoned flour and place in a large kettle. Add 1 cup dry white wine, ½ cup tomato paste and 1 cup chicken stock. Tie 4 peeled shallots, 10 sprigs coarsely chopped parsley, 2 bay leaves and 2 teaspoons crushed thyme leaves in cheesecloth and add to veal. Season to taste with salt and pepper. Cover dish and bring to a boil. Lower heat and simmer until veal is tender (about 45 minutes to 1 hour). Remove cheesecloth bag. If sauce is too thick, thin with additional wine or chicken stock. Correct seasoning; sprinkle finely chopped parsley on top and serve.

COLD LEMON SOUFFLÉ

(8–10 Servings)

Double ingredients used for filling of Lemon Chiffon Pie (recipe page 173) and follow same procedure. Instead of filling tart shell, prepare a 1½-quart soufflé dish as follows: Tie a lightly greased collar of wax paper around outside of soufflé dish so that paper rises 3 inches above top of dish. Fill dish with soufflé mixture to 1½ inches below top of paper. Chill for 2 hours. Remove paper just before serving. Serve with a raspberry or strawberry sauce.

MENU 25

Gazpacho*
Roast Beef
French Bread — Broccoli with Lemon Butter — Red Burgundy
Baked Potatoes
Hearts-of-Palm Salad
Special Chocolate Soufflé*

The Gazpacho is unlike any other I've ever had, and we love it. With a blender to do the work, it couldn't be easier to make, and it freezes well, too. I know that recipes for so-called non-collapsible soufflés do exist, but you won't find one here. When feathers are heavy and flowers cease to be fragile, I may change my mind but, as of now, I think you should ask your guests to wait for the soufflé rather than try to hold it high. This Chocolate Soufflé is truly worth waiting for.

GAZPACHO

(8–10 Servings)

¼ cup almonds, ground (4 tablespoons)
2 shallots, peeled and chopped
1 teaspoon salt
1 teaspoon white pepper
2 eggs
1 cup salad oil
½ cup cider vinegar
1 can (16-ounce) Italian tomatoes
2 medium cucumbers, peeled and chopped
1 teaspoon cloves, ground
1 teaspoon cumin, ground
Cayenne
3 slices stale white bread (crusts removed)
4 cups chicken stock
1 cup heavy cream
Seedless grapes, peeled

Put ¼ cup ground almonds, 2 peeled and chopped shallots, 1 teaspoon salt, 1 teaspoon white pepper, 2 eggs, 1 cup salad oil and ½ cup cider vinegar in blender. Blend until smooth and set aside in a bowl. Put remaining ingredients except grapes in blender and, when smooth, combine them with those in the bowl. Chill. Put 5 or 6 peeled seedless grapes in bottom of each cup; fill cups with gazpacho and serve. (When desired, freeze gazpacho. Add grapes at time of serving.)

SPECIAL CHOCOLATE SOUFFLÉ

(8–10 Servings)

6 ounces dark sweet chocolate
1 cup milk
10 egg whites, stiffly beaten
⅛ teaspoon salt
4 tablespoons confectioner's sugar

Preheat oven to 350°

Melt 6 ounces dark sweet chocolate in top of double boiler with 1 cup milk. Beat 10 egg whites and ⅛ teaspoon salt until foamy; gradually add 4 tablespoons confectioner's sugar and beat until whites stand in peaks. Fold melted chocolate gently into egg whites and pour all into lightly buttered 2-quart soufflé dish. Pile mixture so that center is higher than sides. Bake 30 minutes in preheated 350° oven.

SAUCE

1 cup heavy cream, lightly whipped
3 teaspoons confectioner's sugar
2 teaspoons light rum

Whip 1 cup heavy cream lightly; sweeten with 3 teaspoons confectioner's sugar, and flavor with 2 teaspoons light rum. Serve cream as sauce for soufflé.

MENU 26

Hot Borscht
Blanquette of Veal*
Croissants — Purée of Spinach — Pouilly Fumé
Herbed Rice
Peaches in Red Wine
Gertrude's Topfen Torte*

Blanquette of Veal is one of those dishes that can easily be frozen, so be sure to make more than you need for one meal. Sprinkle a little grated nutmeg on the spinach. Gertrude's Topfen Torte is a lovely cake; the recipe was given to me by a Viennese friend.

BLANQUETTE OF VEAL

(6–8 Servings)

3 pounds young white veal, cut into bite-size pieces
12 small carrots
18 small white onions, peeled
1 teaspoon salt
¼ teaspoon white pepper
Chicken stock
3 tablespoons butter
3 tablespoons flour
¾ pound mushrooms, sliced
3 egg yolks, slightly beaten
Juice of 1 lemon
¾ cup light cream

Soak 3 pounds young veal in cold water for 20 minutes while preparing vegetables. Pour off water and place veal, 12 small carrots, 18 small white onions, 1 teaspoon salt and ¼ teaspoon white pepper in saucepan. Cover meat and vegetables with chicken stock (approximately 4 cups). Cover saucepan and bring contents slowly to boil, skimming from time to time. Let simmer gently for about 1 hour or until meat is tender. Remove meat and keep warm. Remove vegetables and discard. Melt 3 tablespoons butter in skillet, add 3 tablespoons flour and cook for 3 minutes. Add 1 cup hot broth in which veal has cooked (reserving balance of broth for soup stock or sauce at another time) and bring to boil. Add ¾ pound sliced mushrooms and simmer sauce for 10 minutes. Remove from fire and add a little sauce to 3 slightly beaten egg yolks. Blend all together, add juice of 1 lemon, veal* and ¾ cup light cream. Re-heat, but do not boil. Correct seasoning and serve.

* Blanquette may be done to this point the day before and cream added when reheated. It can also be frozen before cream is added.

GERTRUDE'S TOPFEN TORTE

(8–10 Servings)

1¼ cups granulated sugar
10 tablespoons butter (1 bar and 2 tablespoons)
8 egg yolks
1¼ cups dry pot cheese, sieved
1¼ cup almonds, blanched and ground
Grated rind of 1 lemon
1 teaspoon vanilla extract
2½ tablespoons dried white bread crumbs
Salt
8 egg whites, stiffly beaten

Preheat oven to 350°

Cream 1¼ cups sugar with 10 tablespoons butter. Add 8 egg yolks one by one and beat well. Put 1¼ cups dry pot cheese through a sieve and beat into mixture. Add 1¼ cups ground almonds, grated rind of 1 lemon, 1 teaspoon vanilla extract and 2½ tablespoons dried white bread crumbs. Blend all together. Add a pinch of salt to 8 egg whites and beat until stiff. Fold egg whites into batter and pour into lightly buttered and floured 10-inch spring-form pan. Bake 1 hour in preheated 350° oven.

MENU 27

Clam Bisque
Crabmeat Dish*
Italian Bread — Rice — Chablis
Peas
Alligator Pear Salad
Plum Tart

Clam bisque is easily made by heating bottled clam juice and, just before serving, adding a little whipped cream to each cup. The plum tart is made like the Apricot Tart (recipe page 204). I like to use the small blue plums skin side up (after they've been halved and pitted).

CRABMEAT DISH

(8–10 Servings)

½ pound butter (2 bars)
8 large mushrooms, sliced

2 tablespoons shallots, chopped
4 large ripe tomatoes, cut into small squares
2 pounds fresh lump crabmeat
1 teaspoon parsley, chopped
½ teaspoon chives, chopped
½ teaspoon chervil
2 egg yolks
2 cups medium cream
1¼ teaspoon salt
½ teaspoon white pepper
4 tablespoons brandy

Using deep frying pan, heat ½ pound butter. Add 8 sliced mushrooms and cook for 3–4 minutes. Add 2 tablespoons chopped shallots and 4 large tomatoes, cut up; cook 3 more minutes. Add 2 pounds fresh lump crabmeat and let crabmeat heat through, being careful not to break up lumps. Add 1 teaspoon chopped parsley, ½ teaspoon chopped chives and ½ teaspoon chervil. Blend 2 egg yolks with 2 cups medium cream and add to crabmeat. Do not allow to boil. Season with 1¼ teaspoons salt and ½ teaspoon white pepper. Just before serving, heat and flame 4 tablespoons brandy and stir into crabmeat dish. (This dish may also be served cold.)

MENU 28

Hot Madrilène
Cold Poached Salmon, Sharp Sauce*
French Bread — Cucumber Salad — Sancerre
Cheesecake

The Sharp Sauce is from Sweden, where it is frequently served with shrimp or with raw, salted salmon, called Gravlax. The contrast of the colors in the sauce and the poached salmon pleases the eye as much as the contrast in flavors pleases the palate.

COLD POACHED SALMON, SHARP SAUCE

(6–8 Servings)

Using 1 4–5-pound piece fresh salmon, follow directions for poached striped bass given on page 197. When salmon is done, arrange on cold serving platter, add 1 pound cooked shrimp and garnish dish with crisp parsley. (Omit aspic, but reserve strained court-bouillon in which salmon was cooked and freeze it.) Serve salmon and shrimp with following sauce:

SHARP SAUCE

1½ tablespoons Dijon mustard
¼ teaspoon sugar
1 tablespoon lemon juice
1 tablespoon tarragon vinegar
6 tablespoons olive oil
Salt
Freshly ground black pepper
1 cup chopped fresh dill

Blend together all ingredients except dill and beat vigorously. Add 1 cup chopped fresh dill and serve sauce with poached salmon and cooked shrimp.

MENU 29

Mussels Vinaigrette*
Italian Bread — Lamb Pilaf — Tavel
Artichokes, Hollandaise Sauce
Apricot Soufflé, Custard Sauce*

Mussels are delicious prepared this way and they can be done in advance, but they are trouble to clean thoroughly! Serve them only to cherished friends who are known to be mussel lovers. (For this reason, I have written the recipe for two servings.) The Apricot Soufflé has almost no calories and it is unbelievably light. Make the Custard Sauce first so that you will be free to be with your guests when the soufflé goes into the oven.

MUSSELS VINAIGRETTE

(*Note: Recipe given for 2 servings only*)

40 mussels (including possible discards)
2 tablespoons dry mustard
½ cup parsley, chopped fine
½ cup shallots, chopped
2 cups dry white wine

Using a wire brush, scrub mussels clean in cold water. Cover mussels with clean cold water, add 2 tablespoons dry mustard and let stand for 10 minutes. Rinse well and discard any opened mussels. Put mussels in large kettle with ½ cup chopped parsley, ½ cup chopped shallots and 2 cups dry white wine. Cover kettle and steam mussels until shells open. Discard any that do not open. Drain mussels (saving broth in which mussels have been steamed; it should be carefully strained and may be frozen to use as a base for a sauce or soup). Remove top half of shells. If mussels are small, put 2 in bottom half of each shell. Arrange on a flat plate and refrigerate. Before serving, sprinkle the following sauce over mussels:

SAUCE VINAIGRETTE

4 tablespoons light salad oil (not olive oil)
4 tablespoons red wine vinegar
4 teaspoons parsley, finely chopped
Salt
Pepper
2 lemon wedges

Blend all ingredients except lemon wedges together, beating vigorously. Sprinkle over mussels and serve with lemon wedges.

APRICOT SOUFFLÉ, CUSTARD SAUCE

(*6–8 Servings*)

Make Custard Sauce first (recipe pages 195–196).

½ pound dried apricots
1 tablespoon sugar
5 egg whites
Cream of tartar
¼ cup confectioner's sugar

Preheat oven to 350°

Cover ½ pound dried apricots with water and let stand for at least 2 hours or, if possible, overnight. Add 1 tablespoon sugar and cook in same water until soft. Blend apricots smooth in blender or put through coarse strainer. Whip 5 egg whites with pinch of cream of tartar until foamy; add ¼ cup confectioner's sugar gradually and beat until whites stand in peaks. Gently fold apricot pulp into egg whites and pour into lightly greased 1½-quart soufflé dish. (Pile mixture higher in center than on sides.) Bake 30 minutes in preheated 350° oven.

MENU 30

	Fresh Sorrel Soup*	
Croissants	Ham with Madeira Sauce	Pouilly Fumé
	French Peas*	
	Potato Balls	
	Rice Pudding	

This version of Sorrel Soup is quite different from the one given in *My Favorite Things*, but it can only be made when fresh sorrel leaves are available. It's excellent served hot or cold and it freezes well. Rice pudding is another one of those simple desserts that almost everyone enjoys.

FRESH SORREL SOUP

(6–8 Servings)

1 large bunch fresh sorrel leaves
¾ cup onions, chopped
6 tablespoons butter
1½ cups light cream

3 egg yolks, beaten
4½ cups strong chicken stock
Salt
Freshly ground black pepper

Trim, wash and dry a large bunch of fresh sorrel leaves; cut into strips. Sauté ¾ cup chopped onions in 6 tablespoons butter until onions are translucent (but not brown). Add sorrel strips and cook until they are wilted. Combine 1½ cups light cream with 3 beaten egg yolks until well blended. Bring 4½ cups strong chicken stock to a boil, reduce heat and add a little of the hot stock to the cream and egg yolks. Add rest of stock and blend all. Add sorrel-and-onion mixture and season to taste with salt and freshly ground black pepper. Heat thoroughly but do not boil once you have added cream and egg yolks.

FRENCH PEAS

(*6–8 Servings*)

2 packages small frozen peas in butter sauce
1 cup beef stock
3 cans small white pearl onions, drained
1 small head iceberg lettuce
1 teaspoon salt
¼ cup sugar
4 slices prosciutto, cut into small pieces
2 tablespoons flour (if necessary)

Put contents of 2 packages small frozen peas in large saucepan with 1 cup beef stock, contents of 3 cans small pearl onions, lettuce leaves torn from 1 small head iceberg lettuce, 1 teaspoon salt, ¼ cup sugar and 4 slices of prosciutto cut up into small pieces. Cook slowly in uncovered saucepan until peas are tender. If necessary, add 2 tablespoons flour as binder and cook for 2–3 minutes. Correct seasoning before serving.

MENU 31

Lobster Bisque
Linda's Cold Chicken, Lemon Sauce*
French Bread | Mixed Vegetable Salad | White Graves
Apple Pie

Use a drop of red vegetable coloring to make your lobster bisque a faint pink. I find that a very good bisque can be made using frozen lobster tails. Serve a simple oil-and-vinegar dressing on the vegetable salad to balance the creamy sauce of the chicken.

LINDA'S COLD CHICKEN, LEMON SAUCE

(6–8 Servings)

2 3½-pound chickens
2 onions
12 cloves
6 shallots, peeled
3 large carrots, peeled and cut up
8 sprigs parsley
1 tablespoon salt
2 teaspoons peppercorns
Rind of 1 lemon

Put chickens in heavy pot with water to cover; add 2 whole

onions, each pierced with 6 whole cloves, 6 peeled shallots, 3 carrots, peeled and cut up, 8 sprigs parsley, 1 tablespoon salt, 2 teaspoons whole peppercorns and the rind of 1 lemon. Bring to a boil; lower heat and simmer for approximately 1 hour or until chickens are tender. Remove pot from heat and let chickens cool in stock. Remove chickens. Discard skin and pull chicken meat from bones in large pieces. Discard bones. Strain stock and reserve.

LEMON SAUCE

¼ cup lemon rind, grated
Juice of 1 lemon
¼ cup dry sherry
1 teaspoon salt
¼ teaspoon white pepper
1 cup heavy cream
2 egg yolks
¼ cup parsley, minced
1½ cups chicken stock, strained

Bring 1½ cups chicken stock to a boil; add ¼ cup grated lemon rind, juice of 1 lemon, ¼ cup dry sherry, 1 teaspoon salt and ¼ teaspoon white pepper. Cook for 5 minutes. Blend 1 cup heavy cream with 2 egg yolks and add to sauce. Cook over low heat (do not allow to boil), stirring constantly, for 2 minutes or until sauce thickens slightly. Remove from heat and add pieces of chicken to sauce. Arrange in serving dish; cool and refrigerate for 2 hours. Sprinkle ¼ cup minced parsley over all.

MENU 32

Crabmeat Cocktail
Roast Duck, Sour Cherry Sauce*
French Bread — String Beans — Bordeaux
Rice
Raw Mushroom Salad
Vanilla Ice Cream with Crystallized Ginger

The duck can be roasted as in this recipe and then served with any sauce you like. The Sour Cherry Sauce pleases us and is quite unusual. The sharp tang of the ginger goes well with the bland taste of the vanilla ice cream.

ROAST DUCK, SOUR CHERRY SAUCE

(4–6 Servings)

2 4–5-pound ducks
Celery tops from 2 bunches celery
Salt
2 medium white onions

Preheat oven to 450°

Wash ducks in cold water and pat dry inside and out. Salt ducks completely. Fill cavities with celery tops and 2 peeled, whole onions. Truss ducks and place on racks in roasting pan and roast at 450° for 1 hour. Baste ducks every 20 minutes. Reduce heat to 350° and roast for 1 hour longer; continue basting every 20 minutes. Pour off fat and pour remaining drippings into saucepan, scraping brown bits from roasting pan. Carve ducks; arrange legs and wings on a heated platter. Loosen skin from breasts with paring knife and replace in roasting pan in oven to keep warm and to continue crisping of skin. Slice breasts and add to heated platter. Before serving, replace skin trimmed to cover breast slices. Pour a little sauce over all and garnish platter with parsley. Serve additional sauce separately.

SOUR CHERRY SAUCE

2 cups pitted sour cherries (drained)
½ cup dry sherry or vermouth
2 tablespoons cornstarch
4 tablespoons chicken stock
Drippings from roasting pan (after fat has been poured off)
1 cup chicken stock

Dissolve 2 tablespoons cornstarch in 4 tablespoons chicken stock and add to ½ cup wine and drippings. Stir and heat until well blended and thickened. Strain sauce. Add 2 cups sour pitted cherries, and serve with duck.

TO MAKE DUCK SOUP

Put remainder of duck carcasses with necks, hearts, livers and 2 teaspoons salt in 2 quarts water. Bring to a boil, then simmer for 1 hour. Strain and, if desired, freeze to be used either as broth or as base for sauce.

MENU 33

Wine Soup*
Italian Bread — Eggs Mollet with Ham in Aspic* — Iced Coffee
Russian Dressing
Coleslaw*
Coeur à la Crème with Blueberries

I've repeated the recipe for the Wine Soup from *My Favorite Things* because it is an original and we like it so much. The Eggs Mollet provide a change from the more usual poached eggs.

WINE SOUP

(Repeated from *My Favorite Things*)

(*8 Servings*)

4 or 5 leeks
1 large onion
1½ bunches watercress
1 large potato
2 cups chicken broth
1½ cups dry white wine
1½–2 cups light cream
Salt
Pepper
2 tablespoons finely cut chives

Cut off and discard all the green part of 4 or 5 leeks. Slice off and discard all the root ends. Split remaining white portions of leeks lengthwise and wash thoroughly. Cut fine; set aside. Peel and chop fine 1 large onion; set aside. Wash 1½ bunches fresh watercress, discarding stems; set aside. Peel, cut and slice fine 1 large potato. Place leeks, onions and potato in pan and add 2 cups chicken broth. Cook until soft (20 to 25 minutes). Add 1½ cups dry white wine and bring to a boil. In a separate pan, cook the watercress in 1½ cups slightly salted boiling water for 2 or 3 minutes. Add this to soup, cool slightly and run it through blender. When cool, refrigerate and, before serving, add as much light cream as desired (1½–2 cups). Adjust seasoning to taste. Serve in chilled bouillon cups and garnish with a few chives.

EGGS MOLLET WITH HAM IN ASPIC

(*6–8 Servings*)

12 eggs
1 envelope gelatin
2 tablespoons brandy
2 cups beef stock
6 slices boiled ham, ¼-inch thick
Fresh tarragon, finely chopped

Lower 12 eggs into rapidly boiling water. Turn heat down immediately and allow eggs to remain in barely simmering water for exactly 6 minutes. Put eggs under running cold water as soon as time is up. Remove shells carefully (white should be firm, but yolk should not be set). Let eggs stand in cold water while aspic is being prepared.

Soften gelatin in 2 tablespoons brandy; add 2 cups hot beef stock and stir until gelatin is completely dissolved. When aspic is barely set, pour some in bottom of appropriate serving dish. Cut 6 slices boiled ham into julienne strips and arrange over aspic. Arrange eggs on top of ham; top eggs with finely chopped tarragon and spoon aspic over all.

COLESLAW

(6–8 Servings)

1 large green cabbage
2 large carrots

Shred cabbage coarsely; peel and grate 2 carrots. Mix together in a large bowl and add the following dressing:

1½ cups mayonnaise
½ cup onion, finely chopped
¼ cup light cream
2 tablespoons caraway seeds
½ cup fresh dill, chopped fine (or 2 tablespoons dried dill weed)
Salt
Pepper

Mix all ingredients until well blended. Add to cabbage and carrots and toss until vegetables are coated with dressing.

MENU 34

Boula Soup
Paillard of Veal
Rye Bread Toast — Spatzeles* — Beer

String Beans with Sour Cream and Caraway Seeds
Bib Lettuce Salad
Ginger Roll with Ice Cream*

The Boula Soup is another "easy to make" blending of canned varieties—turtle soup and pea soup. Add a little sherry and, just before serving, top with a little whipped cream and put under the broiler. The paillard is merely a well-pounded scallop of veal, quickly grilled. When it's done, add a bit of lemon-flavored butter, salt and pepper and some chopped parsley. Garnish platter with watercress. The Ginger Roll can, of course, be made in advance and frozen.

SPATZELES

(8–10 Servings)

3 eggs
3 egg yolks
1½ cups milk
3 cups flour, sifted
1½ teaspoons baking powder
1½ teaspoons salt
¾ teaspoon white pepper
Grated nutmeg
6 tablespoons butter, melted
2 quarts chicken stock
¼ pound butter, melted (1 bar)
Freshly ground black pepper

Beat 3 eggs with 3 egg yolks and add milk. Sift 3 cups flour, 1½ teaspoons baking powder, 1½ teaspoons salt, ¾ teaspoon pepper and some grated nutmeg into mixing bowl. Add 6 tablespoons melted butter to flour and add egg-and-milk mixture slowly, stirring constantly. Strain batter if necessary to remove lumps. Bring 2 quarts chicken stock to a boil and drop in ¼ teaspoons of batter (about 10 at a time). Cook for 2–3 minutes or until spatzeles rise to surface. Remove them with slotted spoon as soon as they are done and put them in a collander under cold running water while continuing to cook balance of batter. When making spatzeles in advance, keep them in cold water in refrigerator until ready to serve. At that time, re-heat chicken stock in which spatzeles were cooked, drain spatzeles and heat through in stock. Drain thoroughly and put into heated serving dish. Pour ¼ pound melted butter over all and season to taste with salt and freshly ground black pepper.

GINGER ROLLS

(8 Servings)

⅓ cup butter
⅓ cup granulated sugar
⅓ cup molasses
1 cup flour
1 teaspoon baking soda
1 teaspoon ginger
1 teaspoon cinnamon
1 teaspoon allspice
1 teaspoon nutmeg
½ cup hot water
1 beaten egg
Confectioner's sugar
1 pint softened vanilla ice cream

Preheat oven to 375°

Melt ⅓ cup butter and mix with ⅓ cup sugar and ⅓ cup molasses. Put flour, baking soda, spices, beaten egg and ½ cup hot water in bowl and combine with molasses mixture, beating lightly until blended. Lightly oil a jelly-roll pan 13½ x 9½ x 1 inch deep. Line the pan with waxed paper, leaving ends of paper extending about 4 or 5 inches. Lightly oil paper. Spread mixture on paper evenly and bake in preheated 375° oven until set (about 12 to 15 minutes). Remove from oven, cover with cloth wrung out in cold water, cool 5 minutes, then chill in refrigerator for 25 minutes longer.

Put overlapping sheets of wax paper on kitchen table. Dust paper with confectioner's sugar to approximate size of jelly-roll pan. Remove pan from refrigerator and towel from top of roll and turn roll out onto sugared paper. Gently remove the wax paper on which roll was baked. Spread with 1 pint softened vanilla ice cream and roll up lengthwise, using paper to help shape roll. Holding ends of paper, lift roll onto platter. Cut off ends of paper. Chill roll in refrigerator or freeze in freezer. When ready to serve, sprinkle with confectioner's sugar.

MENU 35

Prosciutto and Melon
Chicken à la Reine*
French Bread — Broccoli Fleurettes — White Burgundy
Barley Casserole
Mixed Green Salad
Crème Caramel

The prosciutto is equally good with fresh pears or figs. Barley is a nice variation from potatoes, rice and pasta.

CHICKEN À LA REINE

(6–8 Servings)

4 whole chicken breasts, halved and boned
Flour
Salt
Pepper
12 tablespoons butter, clarified (1½ bars)
2 chicken bouillon cubes
1 cup dry sherry
3 cups heavy cream
½ teaspoon Maggi
2 tablespoons lemon juice

Skin 8 half chicken breasts and cut into large bite-size pieces (about 1½ inches square). Dust chicken with seasoned flour and sauté in 12 tablespoons clarified butter over high heat until chicken whitens. (Do not brown.) Crush 2 chicken bouillon cubes and add them to pan. Heat and flame sherry and pour over chicken. Turn heat very low, add 3 cups heavy cream and simmer for about 15 minutes. Add ½ teaspoon Maggi. If sauce is too thick, thin with a little milk. Before serving, squeeze 2 tablespoons lemon juice over all.

MENU 36

Canapé of Steak Tartar with Fresh Caviar
Chicken in the Pot with Matzo Balls*
Rye Bread Toast Tomatoes and Okra Vouvray
Strudel with Cheese Filling

For the steak tartar, double grind some prime top sirloin from which all fat has been removed. Season with salt, pepper, a little chopped onion and a few drops of Worcestershire Sauce. (I sometimes beat a raw egg and add it as a binder to about 1 pound of beef.) Spread beef on toast and top it with a thin layer of caviar. The two flavors complement each other beautifully. For the strudel, use a commercially prepared strudel dough or phyllo, and take your pick of any number of glorious fillings—from apple, the most often used, to cheese or poppy seed or prune.

CHICKEN IN THE POT

(8–10 Servings)

2 3-pound fryers
4 cups chicken stock
1½ tablespoons salt
1 teaspoon whole black peppercorns
4 large carrots, scraped and sliced
3–4 large leeks, trimmed
1 bunch celery, including tops
6 sprigs parsley

Wash 2 3-pound fryers in cold water and pat dry. Put them in large kettle with 4 cups chicken stock and enough cold water to cover. Add 1½ tablespoons salt, 1 teaspoon whole black peppercorns, 4 scraped and sliced carrots, 3–4 trimmed leeks, 1 bunch celery (with tops) and 6 sprigs parsley. Bring to boil. Skim. Cover pot and allow to simmer for 1 hour or until fryers are tender. (Juice in chicken legs should be clear when leg is pierced with fork.) Remove fryers and keep them warm. Skim fat from top of broth and strain. Discard vegetables. Pour liquid into pot, correct seasoning and, while carving chickens, boil matzo balls in soup for 5 minutes. Place carved chickens in heated tureen, pour soup and matzo balls over all and ladle into deep soup dishes. To be served as a main course.

MATZO BALLS

(*makes 18–20*)

2 tea matzos, broken up
1 small white onion, finely chopped
1 tablespoon butter
1 egg, beaten
1 tablespoon matzo meal
1 tablespoon parsley, chopped
¼ teaspoon salt
Monosodium glutamate

Soak 2 tea matzos in warm water just to cover for 10 minutes. Squeeze out all water. Sauté 1 small chopped onion in 1 tablespoon butter until onion is translucent. Add onion, 1 beaten egg, 1 tablespoon matzo meal, 1 tablespoon chopped parsley, ¼ teaspoon salt and a dash of monosodium glutamate to the 2 tea matzos and mix well. Refrigerate for at least 30 minutes. Roll into balls about 1 inch in diameter and drop them 3 or 4 at a time into boiling chicken soup so that soup does not stop boiling. Boil for 5 minutes and remove. When all are done, replace balls in soup and keep hot until time to serve. Allow 2 or 3 balls to each serving of chicken in the pot or of Home-Style Chicken Soup (recipe page 187).

January 1967

NOW the house is finished; we are living in it and we love it. But I promised to write an "If Only . . ." chapter and to be completely honest about it. I hoped it could be short—and it will be, for which I'm very thankful. But it would be less than honest for me to pretend that the few "if only's" are minor or unimportant. Two of them cannot possibly be corrected or changed, and the third would entail such vast cost that it would be completely unrealistic to try to do so.

If only we had known how much confusion, delay, uncertainty and expense we would have to accept, we would never have asked for the kind of ultra-sophisticated system of heating and air-conditioning that we have. While everything about the aesthetics of the house—the planning, the execution, the result—has been a joy, mechanics have been a nightmare from start to finish. From the first, everyone concerned blamed somebody else. No one accepted the responsibility for motors that were quite literally hooked up to run backward or wiring that was done incorrectly. Before the air-conditioning was turned off for the winter, the lights dimmed throughout the house and whenever the big unit went on, it made a great deal of noise. As I write this, we still hope that it can all be made to work smoothly, and we are assured that it will; but until summer we can't be certain.

After endless delays, hundreds of brilliant double-talk explanations, bewildered experts who came at night or over weekends when things seemed to go wrong for our own special delight (during the week, when we were in New York, we would receive the most reassuring reports), the system is at long last beginning to work. But it really hasn't been worth the wear and tear on our emotions and on the bank account. A less delicate system that did not demand such expertise would have pleased us more, I'm sure.

My second "if only" involves the switches that control the lights throughout the house. They are, in many cases, illogically placed, and I doubt that I will ever learn what turns what on. In some small areas three switches perform the same function; in our long bedroom hall, however, instead of being able to turn the lamp lights on and off outside our bedrooms, we must walk to the far end of the hall to accomplish this. I find myself playing hide and seek a good deal with the rheostats; they do the hiding and I the seeking. Lights that were supposed to go on automatically when closet doors were opened work that way sometimes, but, in many instances, the lights have separate switches which must be manually operated. To turn on some of the outdoor lights, we have to go into a coat closet . . . and so it goes. This may sound like a small problem, but it is a constant one, and irritating.

Still, I did promise a *chapter* on the "if only's"—"if only we had" or "if only we hadn't"—and now I find myself in the embarrassing position of not being able to fulfill my promise. There are, quite simply, not enough "if only's" for a chapter. Our pleasure in having the house turn out to be so very nearly perfect for us has managed, however, to create one last "if only"—the most important of all and one that cannot possibly be changed, the one that puts everything else into proper perspective: if only we had built the house ten years ago . . .

INDEX

AND

INDEX OF RECIPES

Index

(INDEX OF RECIPES FOLLOWS)

Index of Recipes